DANGEROUS SOCIETY

by
Carl S. Taylor, Ph.D.

Michigan State University Press
East Lansing, Michigan
1990

Copyright © 1989 Carl S. Taylor

All Michigan State University Press books are produced on paper which meets
the requirements of American National Standard of Information Sciences—
Permanence of paper for printed materials
ANSI 239.48-1984.

Michigan State University Press
East Lansing, Michigan 48823-5202

Printed in the United States of America

Library of Congress Cataloging-in-Publication Data

Taylor, Carl S.
    Dangerous society / by Carl S. Taylor.
        p   cm.
    ISBN 0-87013-277-6 (alk. paper)
        1. Gangs—Michigan—Detroit—Case studies.   I. Title
HV6439.U7D67   1989
364.1'066'0977434—dc20   89-43115
                                                                       CIP

Dedicated to my parents, Mae and Gene,
for giving me the best education.

CONTENTS

PREFACE

There are many individuals who made contributions to this project and deserve thanks. My deepest gratitude and appreciation to Lucille Lewsader for typing, to Dr. Sally Pratt for editing the rough draft and her suggestions for the educational component of the CTE, and to Errol Henderson for his assistance with the typology. Special thanks to the staff of the MSU School of Criminal Justice and its director, Dr. Robert Trojanowicz, along with Dr. Dennis Payne for sharing his past experiences of a very distinguished career with the Michigan State Police. Sincere gratitude to Sgt. Anthony Holt of the Wayne State University Public Safety Department for his dedication, patience, and professionalism.

Thanks to the Michigan State University Press: Lori Lancour; Lynne Brown for her diligence in photography and graphics; Julie Loehr for all the extra yards of quality, understanding, and superb directing of everything when it looked hopeless; and Dr. Richard Chapin, Director of the Press, for taking this project and being the hammer I needed to make this book happen.

Many thanks to Dr. George R. Fleming for his views on the past social theories concerning this project and to the investigators, interviewers and researchers in Detroit who gave me an up-front, in-the-trenches perspective. Special thanks to Timothy Mitchell, Kim James, Larry Campbell, Harrison W. Watkins IV, Ronald Hughley, and Nan Houston. Thanks to

Detroit, to Jack Surrell, Earl Van Dyke, Thomas "Beans" Bowles Sr., and Ted White Sr. for sharing the rich past of African-American culture, and to Vincent Piersante for being the historian with compassion from the eyes of a true centurion.

Thanks to all of my family for their support during this process of putting it together: Florene, Floyd, Eva, Ethel, Al, Shawn, Allen, Gene II, and all those I can't name, along with William Sparks for his views of the youth culture in Detroit and Virgil A. Taylor for his keen leadership during the field research and review of this data. My gratitude to Dolores and Dr. Clifton Wharton for role modeling by example and leadership. And finally, special thanks to my past teacher, Paul Stark Seeley, whose wisdom continues, to Ronald Hunt, and to David C. Driver, my dear friend, whose support has been priceless.

Carl S. Taylor

FOREWORD

A reader will not get very far into *Dangerous Society* before it becomes obvious that Carl Taylor knows what he is talking about. His study of Detroit gangs—their evolution, composition, goals and influence on crime and drugs—has the solid ring of truth. It is a professional study, yet it is marked with understanding and compassion that emphasizes the human element and the terrible waste of talent and lives.

These conclusions are not surprising in any work by Carl Taylor. They are, in fact, characteristic of his careful, thorough approach that has been evident to me in the nearly 20 years that I have known him.

Soon after I became president of Michigan State University in 1970, I established a Presidential Fellows program. The idea was to afford a very select group of undergraduate and graduate students and junior faculty members an opportunity to view university administration from the inside. Carl was the first of two undergraduate students selected by the MSU Trustee Selection Committee and me to participate in the program.

Carl's own disadvantaged background in Detroit made him an unlikely candidate for admission to MSU, much less as a Fellow in the program. But his potential was obvious from the outset. Of all the Presidential Fellows with whom I worked over the years, I can truly say that Carl showed the greatest personal and intellectual growth during the fellowship.

He literally soaked up everything to which he was exposed, and yet he never lost the ability to understand and communicate with his fellow students from similar disadvantaged backgrounds. These are the attributes that emerge so clearly in his study, *Dangerous Society.*

Soon after receiving his bachelor of science degree, Carl was hired by the MSU Office of Student Affairs and put in charge of the Minority Aide program in the campus's vast resident hall complex. At the time, the program was in a state of great disarray, but under his leadership over the next several years, he developed it into a model that has been emulated nationally.

There were numerous other areas where his administrative and leadership skills proved to be invaluable, ranging from defusing racially-charged incidents to coping with the student uprisings during the early 1970s.

Carl went on to earn two more degrees from MSU: master of science in criminal justice, and a Ph.D. in administration and higher education with a cognate in criminal justice.

Despite his subsequent success in the private business sector, Carl felt a deep sense of obligation to the basic principles and values of higher education and to his society. He therefore returned to the academic world, and as *Dangerous Society* proves, we are the better for it.

Clifton R. Wharton, Chairman and CEO
Teachers Insurance and Annuity Association—
College Retirement Equities Fund

America is experiencing a serious problem with urban youth gangs. A sharply increasing number of teenagers are becoming involved in the deadly business of drug trafficking—and murdering to protect that business. To date, our institutions have not been equal to the challenge. The traditional juvenile justice system was designed to deal with lesser infractions of the law. The American public and elected legislative bodies need to realistically assess a variety of interrelated problems and waste no time in solving them.

This book focuses on gangs in inner-city Detroit, but many urban centers are experiencing similar problems. In fact, no community in America—urban, suburban, or rural—has escaped the far-reaching effects of drug-related crime. No one is immune. Everyone needs to be aware of what is happening and what needs to happen.

HISTORY

Gangs have existed in the United States since the Revolutionary War. The infamous Jean Laffite led his band of buccaneers against the British in Louisiana in support of General

1

Andrew Jackson. Countless gangs rode during the early days of the Wild West. The Younger Gang and the still-infamous James Gang (Frank and Jesse) were legendary in the history of the West.

The origin of serious youth gang development is rooted in the shift from agrarian to industrial society. Gangs of young toughs were plentiful in early urban America. From the early 1900s to the mid-1930s, industrial cities experienced drastic population increases. Immigrants filled the ghettos of New York and other eastern cities in the early 1900s with groups of youngsters socializing in their respective neighborhoods. Compared with the industrialized states of the east, southern and midwestern states have had smaller teenage populations and less economic growth, consequently, gang growth has been less rapid.

Detroit is a microcosm of urban America. As the cornerstone of the auto industry, this northern city represents the successes and woes of a changing world economy. Detroit has been devastated by urban flight and major job losses. Other cities, such as New York, Chicago, Oakland, Flint, and Saginaw, parallel Detroit with its eroding tax base, economic depression, swelling welfare rolls, poor public education, and skyrocketing crime. As a northern industrialized city, Detroit represents a fight for survival in the face of changing foreign auto competition, a fight that includes finding work for unemployed, unskilled laborers. For the past ten years, the unemployment rate of Detroit has exceeded the national average; many residents have been driven out of state in search of employment. Today's urban young people are unable to find jobs at the auto plants as did their fathers during the flourishing 1960s. Consequently, urban gangs have replaced Ford, GM, and Chrysler as major employers. Social conditions created by industrialization are now producing criminalization.

Youth gangs have existed in Detroit and other major U.S. cities for a long time. As immigrants entered America, Detroit attracted foreign and domestic job seekers to fill the demand for well-paying jobs. Detroit experienced rapid growth during the 1920s, 1930s and, with the industrial needs of World War II, even more in the 1940s and 1950s. Henry Ford lured workers to his newly created auto assembly lines with the promise of $5.00 a day—twice the going factory rate.[1] The unskilled labor required for the assembly line attracted large numbers of ethnic groups. These groups segregated into pockets throughout the city—Polish, Irish, Hungarian, Italian, Finnish, Chinese, blacks—and maintained their own languages and subcultures. The pressure of old values and traditions forced many immigrants to band together to fight the prejudices found in their new environment. Territorial lines were drawn based on race, ethnicity, and religion. Early 1900 Detroit presented a classic example of ethnic segregation. Darden's *Detroit: Race and Uneven Development* suggests that foreign immigrants lived daily as if they were still in their respective countries where the languages and cultures of the Old World continued.[2]

Friction thus arose when these invisible ethnic boundaries were crossed. As predator groups began to invade the territories of others, merchants and businessmen fell victim to extortion and robbery from outside—and sometimes even by members of their own ethnic group. Many youth gangs were originally formed during the early days of industrialization in order to "protect" merchants. Foreign immigrants had very few options since their language and cultural barriers left no other means of assistance. The police were viewed as outsiders—a view still held by many ethnic groups today.

During the 1930s, researchers in Chicago studied ethnic gangs. Frederick Thrasher, a leading authority on gang behavior and author of the 1936 book, *The Gang*, emphasized that gangs often began as play groups within economically poor ethnic neighborhoods.[3] Youngsters who lived together, went to school together, and participated in neighborhood activities together developed a strong sense of identity. They then formed groups within groups that became more cliquish and close knit. Gangs that had divergent interests were formed, and the attitude of "us" versus "them" developed. When one group posed any type of threat, it became standard to "protect one's turf."

One of the best examples of a protective youth group was the Jewish gang known as the Sugar House Gang, formed to protect Jewish merchants in the 1920s by Harry and Louis Fleisher and Irving Milberg. Greed, however, drove them to join forces with Norman Purple and his group to form the

Purple Gang. A distilling operation on the north side of Detroit brought in steady cash; extortion, stick-ups, and hijackings became their new trade.

Prior to 1920—and prior to the formation of Detroit's Purple Gang—America had no national crime syndicate. Previous organized crime operations had taken advantage of Detroit's rapid growth and change, but no interstate, national, or international network existed. The Purple Gang was instrumental in building the foundation of Detroit's organized crime syndication. The bootleg liquor industry of Prohibition propelled the Purples into major crime with notable connections beyond Detroit. Alcohol made millions of dollars for organized crime.

Though numerous urban youth gangs came and went during the 1920s, 1930s, and 1940s, the Purple Gang was the dominant, most highly organized gang of that era in Detroit. Today, a great number of youth gangs have become just as organized and just as deadly.

GANG TYPES

Gangs may be primarily defined within three different motivational categories: scavenger, territorial, and corporate. An evolving or maturing gang will embody scavenger and territorial gangs as growth phases of an organized/corporate gang.

Scavenger Gangs

Members of these gangs often have no common bond beyond their impulsive behavior and their need to belong. Leadership changes daily and weekly. They are urban survivors who prey on the weak of the inner city. Their crimes are usually petty, senseless, and spontaneous. Often, acts of violence are perpetrated just for fun. They have no particular goals, no purpose, no substantial camaraderies. Scavenger gang members generally have the characteristics of being low achievers and illiterates with short attention spans who are prone to violent, erratic behavior. The majority come from the lower class and the underclass.

4

Fredrick Thrasher established that gangs, which evolved from neighborhood play groups, were bonded together without any particular purposes or goals. Thrasher's fifty-year-old study continues today to accurately describe scavenger type gangs. Scavengers are generally poor students and misfits with a low self-esteem who commit any number of crimes in addition to car theft, breaking and entering, and vandalism. Scavenger behavior is characterized by impulsive, erratic, chaotic acts.

Recently, Vincent Piersante, former head of Michigan's Attorney General Organized Crime Division, observed that most gang members who start out in scavenger gangs, later begin professional lives of crime. Thrasher identified specific factors that shape gang behavior, such as the significant role the community can play. He found that the environment is "permissive, lacks control, and facilitates gang activity. The presence of adult crime within these communities also influences gang behavior because many of the adults who have high status in the community are adult criminals."[4]

Sociologist Robert Merton's "strain theory" discusses how a desire for certain goals (e.g., car, money, status) pressures individuals into seeking unacceptable means of acquiring those goals.[5] In the case of scavenger gangs, they become isolated from mainstream society. Most of the urban youth gangs that have existed since early America have been scavenger gangs—groups of youngsters drawn together simply by environment and circumstances. As in the early 1920s, Detroit gangs were Polish, Jewish, Sicilian, or other ethnic groups. The socioeconomic conditions of Detroit created an atmosphere conducive to scavengers.[6]

Shaw and McKay's theory of "cultural transmission" concludes that disadvantaged environments, lack of social controls, and learning passed from one group to another about crime leads youngsters to criminal activities.[7] Vincent Piersante confirmed this theory based on twenty-five years' experience in the Detroit Police Department: "All of these gangs start out small, bonded together as low achievers, misfits, committing small petty crimes. However, if they become successful they gain money and with money comes power—power to influence, power to purchase, and power that brings about status."[8]

Territorial Gangs

A territorial gang, crew, group, or individual designates some thing, some place, or someone as belonging exclusively to the gang. The traditional definition of territory as it relates to gangs is better known as "turf."

When scavenger gangs become serious about organizing for a specific purpose, they enter the territorial stage. During this stage, gangs define themselves and someone assumes a leadership role. It is the process of shaping, forming, and organizing with particular objectives and goals.

Once the gang has defined its territory, the next step is to defend that territory from outsiders. In the process of defining and defending territory, gangs become "rulers." They act as controllers. In the streets, territorial law is more respected and feared than is legal, traditional law. It is well-known and accepted by most that gang law is, in fact, the law in that particular territory.

Gangs defend their territories in order to protect their narcotic business. The word is out on the street to everyone: "This is gang territory—stay away." Each street corner, dopehouse, salesperson, distributor, or customer is part of the territory. Anyone who attempts to enter the territory becomes the invader, the intruder, the enemy. Unlike the legitimate business world, gangs use physical violence as their only enforcement tool to stop competition and opposition. All gang types in this study respect the conditions of territorial law and the necessity that it generates for punishment.

The concept of territory is not new for youth gangs; neither is violence. The gangs in this study reflect contemporary times. Drugs and violence, rooted in the underworld, have propelled them into major crime, creating an outlaw culture employed by the narcotics industry—an industry generating substantial money and, therefore, substantial power. This power allows them to become mobile, and this mobility leads to the expansion of territorial boundaries beyond the few blocks of their respective neighborhoods.

Mobility through financial power is the distinguishing factor between the traditional definition of territory and the nontraditional concept of territory. The classic movie *West Side Story* gave the world a disturbing picture of two urban youth gangs battling over turf: the Sharks defended their neighborhood honor and the Jets defended their territory. But those territory lines were confined to neighborhood ethnic boundaries; they did not have access to large amounts of money nor to the mobility and freedom it could purchase.

Similarly, the gangs of the 1950s, 1960s, and 1970s, particularly scavenger gangs as Detroit youth gangs were then, simply did not have cars. Prior to the windfall of illegal drug profits, territory as a concept was limited to the immediate neighborhood. Today, with the power of organized crime, technology, and escalating wages, territory can be intrastate, interstate, or international.

Organized/Corporate Gangs

These well-organized groups have a very strong leader or manager. The main focus of their organization is participation in illegal money-making ventures. Membership is based on the worth of the individual to the organization. Promotion inside the infrastructure is based on merit, not personality. Discipline is comparable to that of the military and goals resemble those of Fortune 500 corporations. Different divisions handle sales, marketing, distribution, enforcement, and so on. Each member understands his or her role and works as a team member. Criminal actions are motivated by profit. Unlike scavanger gangs, crimes are committed for a purpose, not for fun. Although they have members from lower classes and the underclass, middle-class and upper middle-class youths are also attracted to this type of gang.

The famous Forty-two Gang of Chicago was a textbook example of scavenger/territorial to corporate/organized evolution. In 1931, two University of Chicago sociologists did an in-depth study of this gang of forty-two tough juveniles who were aggressive, reckless scavengers.[9] Though they had no set agenda, they murdered robbery victims, stool pigeons, and police. Considered the worst juvenile gang produced in the United States, the Forty-two Gang was certainly the best "farm team" Chicago's Capone mob ever had. They were ready to do anything for a quick buck. They stripped cars, robbed cigar stores, marched into nightclubs and staged holdups, and killed horses, hacking off their hind legs to supply certain outlets with horsemeat.

Eventually some of the 42ers graduated into the lower ranks of the Capone mob, a well-organized group of adult criminals. Some of the older gangsters viewed them with caution because of their wild, reckless, amoral attitudes. Although they were impressed by the 42's brazen acts, some felt they were "too crazy" for organized work. Over thirty of the forty-two were maimed, killed, or sent to prison for murder, armed robbery, or rape—a primary gang pastime.

Their desire to impress the Capone mob eventually paid off. Many times they would pull off big robberies and leave the word on the street that it was the 42s. They would spend their prized loot at Capone's favorite hangouts. Sam Giancana, who eventually became head of Chicago's crime family, was a 42, as were Sam Battaglia, Sam DeStevano, Rocco Potenza—all of these juveniles came from westside Chicago's "Little Italy."

Gang Players

The individuals or players involved with today's gangs, like the gangs themselves, have distinct motivations, identities, and roles.

Corporate—a person whose main purpose is pursuit of monetary gain. Criminal activities are used by corporate gangs as a means of achieving goal(s).

Scavenger—a person who lives off the environment; survival by means of criminal activities; loosely organized; no definite leadership.

Emulator—a person who emulates gang behavior; dresses or pretends to achieve goals of real gangs. Emulators sometimes truly believe themselves that they are members of real gang organizations. They are on the outside of gang organization. They are pretenders who are not generally accepted by gang members.

Auxiliary—gang members who hold limited responsibilities in corporate gangs. Auxiliary membership is very common for females. These members usually do not participate in all aspects of gang business. This position is also part of testing or auditioning potential members for added responsibilities or full member privileges.

Adjunct Member—members who are part of an organization from a limited membership. These members are permanent part-timers by choice. Sometimes they have relinquished full membership from the organization. Independent business relationships are adjunct for some members. They are protected and regarded as members by outsiders. Some adjuncts have full-time legal jobs and remain adjunct as it relates to criminal commerce.

NEAR-GROUPS

Lewis Yablonsky's definition of gangs differed from that of Thrasher. Yablonsky labeled gangs as near-groups, stating that they fall between mobs and a cohesive group. In *Gang as Near-Group,* Yablonsky states that his definition is based on the unstable, changing, and stable permanent characteristics of the near-group.[10] Yablonsky's near-group possesses "chameleon-like quality." Later, he expanded near-group to describe "violent gangs," those gangs formed to provide emotional gratification as well as violent gratification.

Yablonsky names two other gang types besides violent gangs: (1) social gangs, and (2) delinquent gangs. Social gangs are historically the tough guys who hang out at soda fountains and participate in athletics, local dances, and rap sessions. Delinquent gangs are mainly organized for illegal activity with social interaction a secondary function.

Yablonsky's descriptions of gang types laid a very strong foundation for the gang types in this study. Organized corporate gangs resemble Yablonsky's delinquent gangs. Scavenger gangs are similar to Yablonsky's social and violent gangs. Thrasher's theory of closeness of play groups fits the scavenger's identity better than that of the corporate type. Yablonsky's near-group defines the ever-changing image, leadership, and purpose of the scavenger gangs. The corporate gang of the 1980s has its roots in Yablonsky's delinquent gang. However, the depth, power, and interrelated gang members' mode of operations make the new corporate gang a different phenomenon.

FEMALES

Data in this study introduce new members in urban youth gangs—females. Interviews with one hundred teen-age females offer data regarding the activities and attitudes of female gang members. Most theories of female delinquency are not very gang-conscious. In fact, they usually ignore gangs and treat female delinquency as a more individual or personal problem.[11]

Klein's *Street Gangs and Street Workers* establishes the foundation for female gangs stemming from male gangs.[12] Traditional theorists have viewed boys as more prone to delinquency than girls, but Gold's *Delinquent Behavior in an American City*[13] depicts female delinquency as much more similar to male delinquency than had generally been believed. The data in this study support Gold's premise; the female factor parallels the overall perspective.

Studies have generally supported the traditional view that females are less prone to delinquency than are males and that girls are not catching up with boys' delinquency rates.[14] This study examines individual females as (1) members of male scavenger and organized corporate gangs, or (2) members of all-female gangs, focusing on aspects such as feminism, poverty, education, and psychology, as well as both traditional and nontraditional values and mores.

DETROIT GANGS

Today the inner city of Detroit faces severe poverty and economic depression triggered by the changes in the auto industry which began in the early 1970s. Similar to earlier ghettos, Detroit is ripe for delinquency, crime, and corruption. In the book, *The Truly Disadvantaged,* Wilson[15] shows that high unemployment rates parallel high crime rates.

Detroit led the nation in homicide rates in 1985, 1986, and 1987. The 1987 juvenile homicide rate in Detroit was the nation's highest. According to Detroit Police Department records, more than 64 percent of all Detroit's violent and property crimes were drug related.[16]

Social conditions have worsened in Detroit in the past decade. Ronald Hunt, a community activist and social worker, discussed the problems of urban youth:

Many of these kids come from homes where their parents don't work. The plant closings have devastated this city. The '60s were tough, but the plants provided good jobs. Without jobs people become hopeless and eventually give up the strong community we once had. . . .

By 1980, according to the authors of *Detroit: Race and Uneven Development,* Detroit's population was 63.1 percent black, of which 40 percent were living below the poverty line.[17] For the past twenty years, black youths have had proportionally higher rates of unemployment than has any other group in the United States.

The menacing problems of drugs has propelled Detroit's youth gang problem into high gear. A local law enforcement agent said,

Dope has given these punks the means to become big operators. They've got guns, cars, fancy clothes, and plenty of girlfriends and lawyers. If they didn't have the money they couldn't recruit more punks at these epidemic numbers. And they got parents and business-type people standing up for them.

Bill Shine, a former Detroit police sergeant, singled out Young Boys Incorporated (YBI) as the most dangerous youth gang since the Purple Gang. This highly organized youth gang grossed $7.5 million weekly, $400 million annually in 1982, according to two federal indictments.[18] Sifakis (1987) documents that the Purple Gang was responsible for at least 500 murders.[19] The YBI death toll is unknown, but undoubtedly would be equally impressive.

It is highly unlikely that a gang like Young Boys Incorporated (whose membership consisted of many former scavengers) could have emerged without money earned from narcotics sales. Gang members not only learned from cultural transmission and association, but they also learned to relish their identities as gangsters. Scavengers and corporate

11

gang members develop a "self-role," as Mead theorized many years ago in his *Self Role Theory*.

The new underclass has been growing since the 1960s. The 1970s and 1980s in Detroit have been years of economic depression. Teen unemployment in Detroit has been record-setting. Most agree that what delinquent ghetto youth have desired has been beyond their means. The theorists believe that the unattainable desires of these youths caused a strain on them, provoking them to find their own way to achieve those desires.[20] Later, in this book, scavengers speak of their reckless determination to achieve the good life, whereas corporate gang members have found the vehicle—drug sales—for realizing their desires.

In an interview of June 29, 1987, Clyde Sherrod, a community interviewer from Detroit, offered the following view:

> *Most of the gangs are childhood buddies from the neighborhood. There's a strong bond between these guys. They wouldn't let outsiders in their group unless someone vouches for them. Each gang has its own personality. Some of the fellas hang together and just hang out. The fellas from the stable families are careful as to what kind of things they get into. The hard core dope boys were learning all the wrong things and many times violent just for kicks. I've seen kids from the same block go two entirely different directions. The small, destructive violent gangs preyed on kids from their own blocks. Sometimes I wondered how the good kids could come from the same block as the crazy ones.*

In the final analysis, scavenger and corporate gangs are somewhat defined by already existing social theories. However, in exploring these two gang types it has become apparent that in Detroit the gang psyche has reached epidemic levels. Although both gang types have roots going back many years, today's youth gangs have reached a new all-time high for deadliness.

Notes
1. George S. May, "The Michigan Automobile Industry to 1945," *Michigan: Visions of Our Past* (Michigan State University Press, 1989): 177.
2. Joe Darden. Joe Darden, June Thomas, and Richard Thomas, *Detroit: Race and Uneven Development (The Report of the Detroit Strategic Planning Project)*, 1987.
3. Frederick Thrasher, *The Gang* (Chicago: University of Chicago Press, 1936).
4. Ibid.
5. Robert Merton, "Social Structure and Anomie," *American Sociological Review* 3, no. 5 (October 1938); Emile Durkeim, *Rules of Sociological Method* (1895) (Glencoe, Illinois: Free Press, 1950). Durkeim was the theorist of anomie—a feeling of isolation from the mainstream of society.
6. Ibid.
7. Clifford R. Shaw and Henry D. McKay, *Juvenile Delinquency and Urban Areas* (Chicago: University of Chicago Press, 1969).
8. Vincent Piersante, interview, April 5, 1988.
9. Carl Sifakis, *The Mafia Encyclopedia* (New York: Facts on File Publications, Inc., 1987).
10. Lewis Yablonsky, "Gang as Near-Group," *Social Problems* 7 (Fall 1959): 108-17.
11. *The Report of the Detroit Strategic Planning Committee*, Detroit Police Records, November 1987.
12. Malcolm W. Klein, *Street Gangs and Street Workers* (Englewood Cliffs, N.J.: Prentice-Hall, Inc., 1971).
13. Martin Gold, *Delinquent Behavior in an American City* (Belmont, Calif.: Brooks/Cole, 1970).
14. The Uniform Crime Reports for the past ten years depict female delinquency as not catching up with their male counterparts.
15. William Julius Wilson, *The Truly Disadvantaged* (University of Chicago Press, 1987).
16. *The Report of the Detroit Strategic Planning Committee.*
17. Darden, et al.
18. Tim Belknap, "Young Boys Inc. Ring—20 Plead Guilty in Dope Trial," *Detroit Free Press*, 3 April 1983.
19. Sifakis.
20. Merton.

THE NEIGHBORHOOD

Inner city Detroit has had a unique socioeconomic layout. During the boom years in the 1940s and 1950s, rich and poor blacks lived in relatively close proximity. Pride and care were evident. Black workers—employed in large numbers by the auto industry—developed strong working- and middle-class neighborhoods. Despite being segregated, these communities showcased black businesses and supported black professionals. Many black southerners migrated to Detroit in search of jobs on the newly developed assembly lines. The 1920s through 1940s were years of racial and ethnic separation and segregation both at the work place and at home.

America's worst race riot occurred in 1943 in Detroit. Until that time, blacks had lived exclusively on the east side. "Paradise Valley" and "Black Bottom" were names that symbolized night life and ethnic boundaries for black Detroiters. After the race riots, segregation began to loosen its grip on blacks. The black migration westward in Detroit was sharply increased in the early 1950s by urban renewal plans. As blacks moved from their east side enclave many black businesses were destroyed.

Thomas Bowles, Sr., a well-respected businessman, musician, and music educator, commented:

15

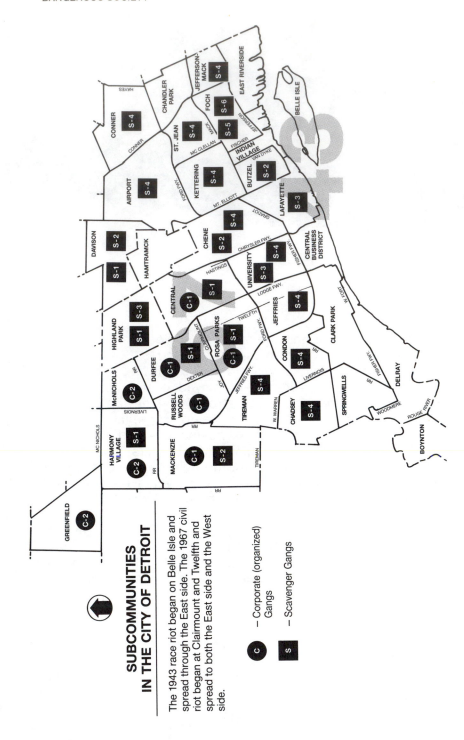

SUBCOMMUNITIES
IN THE CITY OF DETROIT

The 1943 race riot began on Belle Isle and spread through the East side. The 1967 civil riot began at Clairmount and Twelfth and spread to both the East side and the West side.

C – Corporate (organized) Gangs

S – Scavenger Gangs

> *Paradise Valley was a beautiful place. Blacks entertained in black clubs. It was a first-class atmosphere. When they broke up the east side, blacks in a strange way suffered when so-called integration caused businesses to fail. When those bull-dozers tore down Hastings Street the black community shifted over to Twelfth Street and it was never the same. Paradise Valley was ours. . . .*

Black neighborhoods in Detroit became a socioeconomic mosaic on the west side. For blacks, moving to the west side was a climb up the social ladder. However, the social levels ranged from very poor families, classified as the underclass today, to very elite, wealthy families. It was not unusual for poor families to live in crowded, rundown apartments while less than two blocks away some of Detroit's finest homes—not just in the inner city, but in all of Detroit—were occupied by a strong middle class and by upper-middle class black professionals.

THE GANGS

This study was informal, with a no-holds-barred flow of topics covered.

Questions were sometimes posed directly to subjects and at other times were indirect. Once the research team members were able to gain the confidence of gang members, the dialogue was very fruitful. Traditional up-front (open) research methodology could not be used in such risky conditions.

Over a five-year period, the research team conducted more than two hundred interviews with teenagers, female and male, gang and nongang. Additional interaction with various individuals in the community gave the researchers a better understanding of the problems.

Organized corporate gangs in Detroit were represented by two gangs: Gang C-1* with about 300 members and Gang C-2 with less than 100 members. We selected 40 subjects from the ranks of these two groups.

---

*Note: This study does not name gangs nor members by their actual names.

Although there were approximately 100 more members of scavenger type gangs, we selected an equal-sized group of 40 subjects from these groups for our study. Scavenger gangs were represented by four main groups: Gang S-1 with 200 members; Gang S-2 with 100 members, Gang S-3 with approximately 150 members, and Gang S-4 with 50 members. *

The chief field investigator and the principal investigator resided in the working class section of this neighborhood during their youths in the 1950s. This west side neighborhood is the same one that Gangs C-1 and C-2 presently occupy. In the past thirty years, urban youth gangs have emerged as a subculture that society is still trying to define.

THE HISTORY

The investigators from the Gang C-1 neighborhood and other investigators from the same chronological time period compared the evolution of their respective neighborhoods. The C-1 community was a mixture of working class and professionals. In 1958 a west-side gang of notoriety, the "Stompers," allegedly existed, although they seem to have been more myth than reality. There were reports of certain members wearing black leather jackets and bullying students at the local soda fountain. The "Stompers" even had the "Stompettes," their female counterpart. There were constant rumors at school of great gangs invading school grounds. Yet, most of the gangs in the 1950s were almost identical to Thrasher's or Yablonsky's definition of gang member or near-group.

The investigator from the Gang C-1 neighborhood describes gangs:

> They were usually guys from the same streets who skipped school in elementary and who bullied anyone that wasn't from their street or side of town. You knew who they were by the sixth grade easily. They didn't wear jackets, colors, or even have gang names. Sometimes we named them ourselves to distinguish one

---

*These numbers represent gang confederacies as many scavenger members belong to more than one gang.

group from the other. They were usually the best athletes and dumbest students. They would pick on anybody who had money, musical instruments, talked proper, wore clean and nice clothes, were light-skinned, had nice hair, or that would tell teachers on them. They usually numbered around six to nine guys.

These nameless groups ran in packs and survived by committing petty crimes. Gang C-1's neighborhood had social controls that the principal and chief investigators recalled vividly.

My brother and I were community property. At school, teachers were the only word. If a teacher said, "Do it," you did it. If a teacher contacted your parents you were good as gone . . . teachers were always right. If a neighbor saw us walking down the street and requested our assistance, it was done and for free, with a smile. Adults on our street, as was the rule in general, were to be respected and obeyed. This rule was expected of the street boys also. No one was exempt. If and when any youngster bucked this system he or she was exited from the community. There was no tolerance for disobedience.

Neighbors, teachers, merchants, and the church were very much in existence from 1958 to 1968. In July 1967, Detroit experienced another crushing blow to its well-being. A raid by overzealous white Detroit police officers triggered America's worst civil riot. Again, Detroit experienced a very negative incident. Bands of poverty-stricken teenagers roamed the streets looting and burning. One former resident complained,

We sat on the porch and watched as color TVs rolled past our house. Our parents forbidded us to leave the house to riot. We were so pissed. I said, "Everybody else is out there, why can't we go?" My father said, "'Cause we ain't everybody else! We work for things, stealing is wrong!" That was the end of that conversation.

That was the beginning of the end of our neighborhood also. The neighborhood stores owned by the Jews were looted and burned. The drugstore gone, the cleaner gone . . . wasn't anything left. The neighborhood show was torched. When the riots ended so did the neighborhood.

19

Prior to 1968 the Gang C-1 neighborhood had a history of local ruffians, bad boys, street types. Certain blocks were considered "badlands" by regular children. As mentioned earlier, Gang C-1 neighborhood schools were frequented by bluebloods, the elites of the black community: Detroit's first city councilman, the black owners of the only black radio station, drugstore proprietors, physicians, dentists, lawyers, and outstanding civic leaders. These streets inhabited by the wealthy and the working class were interwoven throughout the Gang C-1 neighborhood mosaic. There were brick mini-mansions on five streets; less than a mile west of these prominent streets, the area was overcrowded, poverty-stricken, and had large numbers of young children packed into concrete reservations. These two worlds existed side by side. Many of the "bad boys" came from this squalor.

DRUGS

Detroit's drug history is as interesting as its youth gang history. Generally speaking, Detroit was, on the surface, drug-free prior to 1968, though drug history does date back to 1899. Before 1968 hard-core drugs were invisible to the general public. In 1968 street groups began experiencing drugs like the rest of America. The counterculture, Jimi Hendrix, hippies, flower children, and the Black Power Movement invaded traditional America. As drug use escalated in America, Detroiters found marijuana and heroin seeping into the inner city.

Youth groups were lured into philosophical groups like the Black Panthers and religious organizations like the Black Muslims and Shrine of the Black Madonna. Drugs emerged as did political ideology for black youth. Hanging out, petty crimes, drinking wine/alcohol, and getting high on reefer or heroin was being questioned and challenged by constructive rebellion via a rising social consciousness.

Gang C-1 neighborhood youth packs began to change in 1968. Chemically-relaxed hair, pimpish clothing, and lavish automobiles were being questioned openly by black youth. Urban youth groups or gangs could no longer prey on black peers because, politically, everyone black became "sisters and brothers." Manhood was no longer expressed by committing crimes. What should have been a change for the better was another significant variable in the Gang C-1 neighborhood and Detroit's other declining neighborhoods. Although gang activity decreased, a new problem was created by the infusion of hard drugs—heroin.

Heroin addiction invaded inner-city Detroit in 1968. Heroin addicts brought on a crime spree that even the elite homes of the black "blue bloods" couldn't escape. Addicts were popping up throughout the city like a plague. Though heroin addicts stole from the rich, the preponderance of their thefts occurred in working-class and middle-class homes. While youth gangs disappeared in the Gang C-1 neighborhood, heroin created an army of junkies who preyed on the whole community.

Traditional social controls began to lose effectiveness in the late 1960s. The once-powerful Christian church was being challenged by Islam and the radical political ideologies of socialism, communism, and anti-Vietnam War debates. Schools were rocked by children and parents who had changed and who began questioning the schools, adults, authority, and law enforcement. Suddenly, the black family and the extended family were on the wane. Ronald Hunt, a social worker, commented, "This generation had massive use of drugs by their parents. The social problems of migration and economic loss of jobs caused a strain that is still being felt today in 1988."

Drugs exacerbated problems of decay after the 1967 riots. The lure of joining a gang in the Gang C-1 neighborhood diminished from 1968 to 1971. The bonding, friendship, playing around, and petty crimes stayed the same during the Black Power Movement. Some of the Gang C-1 parents were teenage mothers, some single mothers, some drug addicts, and many were third or fourth generation welfare families.

NEIGHBORHOOD CHANGE

By the early 1970s a new type of parent was emerging in Detroit. New kinds of parents, eroding morals, hard drugs, troubled schools, and changing attitudes about church changed the Gang C-1 community from a close-knit,

21

cooperative network of extended families and friends to a declining, less stable community with no vital organization and transient residents. John Arnold, a resident in the Gang C-1 neighborhood, offered a personal view of thirty years:

> We had block clubs. You could tell the kids, "Get off the grass," and they would say "Yes, sir." We knew the bad ones on our street. They would tell the others, "Not on my street!" Now they all curse you. They'll get the momma and she'll shoot you. The girls talk as bad as the boys. We don't have a block club anymore. People are scared and they don't care.
>
> Now the little young ones is dressing fancy, driving them scooters, and some 'em are driving cars. New big cars, some of the real little ones drive the cars; I know they're only 14 or 15. They look at you and you feel like they just as well kill ya. Kids done changed. Everything is changed. In '64, '65, '66, '67, we had beautiful lawns. Block clubs planted flowers near the street. We sponsored a baseball team, had block parties every summer. Now everybody is staying in the house, got bars on windows. The parents and the kids doing wrong together.

In 1971 the Gang C-1 neighborhood youth gangs were small groups of young boys with street names, with no leadership and no direction in general. Drugs had become part of the subculture. Not unlike other American youth, many Detroit youngsters began experimenting with drugs. Gangs of the mid- to late-1970s were generally faceless groups of misfits who conformed to the standard description for scavenger gangs. The Gang C-1 neighborhood had not produced a solid scavenger named-gang worth recalling for some time.

Two members of the investigative team lived in neighborhoods that had many small groups—semi-gangs—on the east side of Detroit. Youth gangs throughout the city had very little direction or organization until 1975. Then several east-side gangs formed violent scavenger-type gangs. These gangs became feared by their community. Two of them, the Errol Flynns and the Black Killers (BK's), wore fashion clothing that served as their trademark. One gang had a hand signal that symbolized their turf, gang, and attack signal. The expensive, stylish Borsalino hats became the official gang crown for the Errol Flynns.

The evolution of the BK's, Errol Flynns, and Coney Oneys was rooted in earlier east-side youth gangs. While the Gang C-1 neighborhood had no major youth gangs, the east side had a few major scavenger gangs and countless near-groups of juveniles. In both cases, gang members would eventually be prevented from a continuing life of crime by growing older, joining the armed services, getting a job, getting married, or they would find themselves incarcerated.

AG, a 42-year-old disabled worker, belonged to a small gang in the Gang C-1 neighborhood. His summary of urban gang life illustrates the prototype of urban youth gangsterism prior to 1979.

Man, we started real young. Me, my brothers and my cut-buddies lived in some apartments on Tuxedo and Linwood. We go to school to get money when we was young as 10 years old. I'd make all them high yella boys give up their candy and lunch money. Shit, me and my boys didn't get no breakfast or lunch money. My momma put us out early in the morning. So you got food and money however you could get it. Me and my boys all lived in the apartment. . . . We didn't have no real name, we jest skip school and hang out. Use to gamble in the school locker room. Taking people's lunch money was easy. We get their lunch money cause they know we breakin 'em down real quick.

I didn't finish elementary school. School was bogue . . . teachers would be on ya, school was tough. Anyway people would laugh and make fun of me and my brothers 'cause we didn't have clothes. That's another reason I liked jumping kids who thought they had money and was better than us. Me, my brother, and about six partners would hook up with some dudes from the apartments on Dexter and jest kick everybody's ass on Friday at the school yard. When we fought back then, it was with fists one on one. . . . We call you out if you grabbed anything, bottle, stick, brick, whatever. I said, "Be a man, fuck that knife or bottle shit, Fight Me!" Dukes to dukes, but today these crazy punks don't fight with nothing but guns. So I tell my kids, I got three boys, "Come home and get the gun. Everybody got guns, so you got to protect yo'self."

It's different today. In some ways the streets is paying like never before. Now me, I had to go to the white man's army and Vietnam. I didn't want no part of that factory job shit in 1963. Wish I could have got one 'em now, but it's too late. So I tell my boys go for it . . . "Whatever it takes, long as you get some

23

*of that paper, do it!" We use to git high on whatever was avail-
able—wine, whiskey, rum, beer, whatever, smoke some weed,
sniff some glue, get some blow, jest git high, me and my boys.*

*Me and my brothers went to detention when we was 12 and
14. We jest do shit for the hell of it, sometimes we git high
and jest start raising hell for nothin'. Today, my sons belong to
a crew and they makin' it work. . . . If you know the street today
it pays. Back then we was jest hanging out. Doing anything to
survive. Me and my guys use to sing on the corner. . . . Sometimes we hook up with the guys from the other streets and go
skating at the Arcadia, then to White Castle for burgers. Make
all those stuck-up chumps with money give it up. . . . But today
it's some real young dudes making money and they got their
shit together. They got money, lawyers, connections, cars, fine
clothes. They doing it the big way. We was jest neighborhood
cats hanging out with nothing to do and nowhere to go. . . . It's
different now, you can make it and git paid if you got the connections.*

Times were changing, and the city was divided by territorial
boundaries, east side, west side, working class, lower class,
though somewhat interwoven throughout. Teens and older
juveniles participated in neighborhood activities, church,
sports, schools. Gangs and groups of local neighborhood
males varied in degrees of delinquency but the overall
paradigm was the scavenger type.

The new era for urban youth gangs in Detroit started
in 1979. Two young black males in their early twenties
organized Gang C-1, reportedly with $80,000 from the insur-
ance policy of a murdered parent. Their *modus operandi* was
to employ teenagers who would be shielded from serious
prosecution for drug trafficking because of their youth.

The birth of Gang C-1 signaled another dimension of
organized crime and juvenile crime. Within a year, Gang
C-1 members were being emulated not only in their own
neighborhood but throughout the whole city. Wearing
expensive clothing, jewelry, driving high-priced cars, and
being paid huge amounts of money in cash spurred this
youth gang into instant city-wide celebrity status. Scavenger
gang members, along with many street-oriented youngsters,
sought membership in this new and very popular gang.
Suddenly, gangsterism became the norm. Scavenging for

petty crimes and surviving were secondary to the image of Gang C-1. Gang C-1 became the role model that many ghetto youngsters emulated or wanted to emulate. Even young females who historically would not socialize with gang types were admiring and fraternizing with Gang C-1. In a little over ten years, Gang C-1 had impacted their own neighborhood and spread throughout the city as if they were the Roman Legion.

Institutions such as drugstores and movie houses were demolished. Neighborhood children were left idle. Idled males were ripe for picking when Gang C-1 opened shop. Gang C-2 followed, and countless scavenger-type gangs became the minor leagues for training young criminals. Although Gang C-1 was supposedly broken in 1982, its ghost haunts Detroit. Gang C-1 became the king of the hill, the Rolls Royce of youth gangs in Detroit. Interestingly, Gang C-1 was reportedly over 300 strong. Dismantling the gang was spearheaded by 41 federal indictments with 39 convictions. Although the visible Gang C-1 was dismantled, what became of those 260-plus former members? Gang C-1 introduced juveniles into the serious world of adult crime.

The evolution of youth gangs in Detroit pinpoints the Gang C-1 neighborhood. The social theories of Thrasher, Yablonsky, Merton, and Durkheim are accurate in outlining the problems of Gang C-1's community.

By 1979 a new wave of urban youth gangs had emerged. In the next chapter we will reveal the thoughts of some urban gang members. Some of the dialogue will show traditional gang attitudes, however some of the gang members reveal the complex, complicated behavior and attitudes of a new breed of urban gangster. This subculture displays the new and the old ways of urban youth gangs. The findings of this study show that urban youth gangs in Detroit have changed significantly since 1958.

THE STUDY

A particular group of well-dressed, teenage concert patrons at a major concert in July 1980 at Joe Louis Arena in Detroit, Michigan piqued my interest and led to a five-year study of youth groups in Detroit. The purpose of the study was to evaluate Detroit youth groups to determine if Detroit had youth gangs that made any difference to the city.

At that time I was the owner of a private investigation/ security company that provided crowd control and protective services for the Joe Louis Arena, one of the largest venues in the country. I had worked numerous concerts and other major events in Detroit during the late 1970s and early 1980s. The concert performer that day was a very popular black artist. Part of my responsibility was to assess the incoming crowd to determine the best strategies for maintaining an orderly and harmonious atmosphere for all.

The crowd that day was young, mostly black, and mostly urban. While standing at the ground-level backstage entrance, I noticed a caravan of luxury late model limousines parking on Atwater Drive. I mistakenly thought that the stars of the main act had arrived for the concert. To my surprise, a group of youngsters wearing fire-engine red sweatsuits and high-top white leather unlaced gym shoes piled out of the limousines. They appeared to be some sort of club—the identical sweatsuits made them almost look like

27

a high school track team—except for their expensive, gaudy gold jewelry: the cables of gold were incredible.

Many concert patrons were staring and whispering, asking whether the youngsters were members of an entertainment group. I was curious too, having never before seen such expensive jewelry on such young lads. When I asked the limousine company owner about them, I was informed that this was Gang C-1.

The owner looked perplexed as he told me that his drivers were paid up front—in cash. He also explained that an unknown woman had ordered six cars for the concert that day. When his drivers saw how young the group was, they called him to double check their instructions. The owner insisted that the drivers were to collect in cash up front. The youngsters not only paid in full, they also gave the drivers hundred dollar tips. The drivers, who were older men, seemed to be very uncomfortable with their young passengers. One driver remarked:

> Don't like this young boy stuff. I ain't never seen that much money on anybody in all of my days! They forgot an umbrella, a camera, or something. Paid me an extra one hundred dollar bill to go and get the camera. Young kids with big rolls of green money, lots of money like you've never seen. Something is different 'bout these kids—this ain't right. Did they rob a bank? Money like that ain't from no paper route. No, sir, these here boys is serious different! I've seen lots of kids, got kids of my own. . . . I'll be glad when I'm finished with this bunch. They give me the shakes.

Over twenty of the Gang C-1 youngsters walked into the concert as if they owned Joe Louis Arena. I assigned two supervisors to monitor their movements. Conferring with Detroit police officers at the concert, I learned that Gang C-1 was allegedly a gang of drug traffickers. I had seen countless gangs of inner-city youth, but this group was not just another gang of young turks. Two things concerned me regarding Gang C-1. First, each member had an extraordinary amount of cash. At the concession stands they purchased items using large bills from very large moneyrolls.

28

Second, the participants did not act like other youth gangs that I had dealt with at other major events. My concern was particularly aroused because of their aloofness, cool demeanor, and expressionless reaction when questioned by authorities. (Police and security units questioned the gang members during intermission when the mere sight of Gang C-1 seemed to excite various members of the audience.) I knew that I was seeing something unlike any youth group or gang that I had ever seen before.

My curiosity about Gang C-1 increased by the minute. My main questions were: Is this something new as far as gangs are concerned? Where are the members coming from? Where and how does this gang operate? I had seen youth gangs in Detroit over the years, but nothing had aroused my concern or interest like Gang C-1. At this point I decided to see if there were youth gangs that made a major difference to Detroit. I have defined "difference" as follows:

1. Do gang criminal activities conflict with the welfare of Detroit area communities?

2. Has gang modeling achieved city-wide celebrity-like status with notable effects on other teenagers?

3. Do criminal enterprises of gangs openly compete with traditional employment institutions?

4. Does gang activity have a negative social impact on neighborhoods and daily community life?

5. Does the gang or its members interrupt or disrupt educational, social, or family routines?

ORIGIN OF NEW GANGS

Over the previous five years my experience with young people confirmed generally held observations of youth gangs. During major events, especially those that attracted young crowds, gangs had been sporadically disruptive and, at times, violent. Experiences at the downtown venues of Cobo Hall and Joe Louis Arena especially confirmed this. The Detroit police had effectively dealt with most gang problems so that gangs had not added a major problem to our staff's crowd control responsibility. My interest that day was very simple: Gang C-1 was different! That evening I continued to inquire from police, street vendors, patrons, arena workers, anyone who might be able to give me any information on the gang.

The following day I received several tips regarding the composition and operation of Gang C-1. To my surprise, the gang allegedly had a membership of well over one hundred members.

The most startling tip led me back to my own neighborhood of twenty years ago. That tip proved crucial to observing the gang, collecting data, and, eventually, interviewing gang members. I was shocked by the information that Gang C-1 was from my childhood neighborhood. Some of the alleged members lived on my old street. Many of them attended the same elementary, junior high, and high school that I had attended. On September 8, 1980, I selected Gang C-1 as the subject of an in-depth study to determine its significance and uniqueness as a youth gang, and to find out if it made a difference.

INVESTIGATIVE TEAM

Since the gang lived in the inner city, it was important to establish contact without drawing unnecessary attention to ourselves and our project. To accomplish the task, I assembled a team from my own company. Our company had investigative experience in both civil and criminal cases in the inner city. A major plus for this project was that several of our investigators currently lived in or near the Gang C-1 neighborhood. As the principal investigator, I required that members of the field research team be able to move freely about in the community. The people chosen were experienced as investigators and had worked in security at major events that attracted gang types.

Virgil A. Taylor headed the four-investigator research team. Everyone had investigative experience in inner-city affairs through our company, CDS, Inc., a licensed detective firm that retained a variety of clients such as attorneys, insurance companies, retailers, grocers, and private schools. All of the investigators were black, ranging in age from 24 to 33. Race was an important factor because this was a predominately black neighborhood. Outsiders, in particular non-blacks, were treated like foreigners or negative authority figures such as bill collectors, process servers, social workers, or police. The mention of research, pretest, or other academic labels meant little, if anything, in this community.

One of the investigators cautioned that even the pretest questioning of alleged Gang C-1 members could be dangerous if gang members felt threatened. This particular investigator was valuable to the team because of his earlier background as a youth gang member, although not in Gang C-1 or its neighborhood. We delayed contact with gang members to accomplish a preliminary objective: Did Gang C-1 make a difference?

Focusing on the gang's neighborhood, the investigative team interviewed residents, merchants, and school officials. The pretest findings showed that the gang had the characteristics delineated by the definition of "difference." The team had difficulty interviewing a cross section of community members because of a code of ethics (having to do with silence for self-preservation, "omerta") among street people. In canvassing neighborhoods, some residents would not answer questions. Investigators sought answers to ten questions:

1. Do you know of any gangs?

2. How many members?

3. What types of things do they do in the neighborhood? What specifically?

4. Have you ever heard of Gang C-1?

5. Are there any other gangs in the area like Gang C-1? Any other gangs unlike Gang C-1?

6. Are there any gangs at your local school?

7. Do you have any gang members as friends?

8. Are there any gang members in your family?

9. Are any gangs involved in neighborhood crime of significance?

10. Is Gang C-1 the status quo for gangs in your neighborhood? (The investigator often had to explain "status quo.")

The questions were asked over a two-month period. The investigators met weekly for debriefing and sharing of data. They concentrated on various community institutions. Starting on September 14, 1980, the four investigators averaged three interviews each week for a weekly total of twelve. Interviews were held at various times throughout the week and investigators were given flexibility to follow up on anything that seemed relevant. By November 17, 1980, the investigative team had conducted one hundred interviews for the pretest. There were no interviews with Gang C-1 members during the pretest. The results of pretest were conclusive: Gang C-1 made a significant difference.

The pretest established that Gang C-1 was primarily a major drug trafficking gang. Some of the investigators had previously had direct contact with family and friends of some of the gang members. However, by this time the investigative team realized that the gang had a code of silence. It was still premature to attempt any type of direct contact with Gang C-1.

After several meetings, the investigative team brought in a police officer/consultant from the area (not from the Detroit Police Department) who was retained because of his extensive work in law enforcement and private security. He had served as a training consultant and advisor for CDS, Inc. since May 1977. The officer/consultant agreed with the principal investigator's concern over contacting Gang C-1. The decision was made that surveillance would give investigators valuable insight into Gang C-1. Starting on December 3, 1980, the investigative team (I-Team) consisted of four full-time investigators and three part-time investigators who observed the gang in their respective neighborhoods and throughout the metropolitan area. Their hours varied from week to week but their observation included gang members' daily routines seven days a week for six months.

Although the investigators attempted no direct contact with Gang C-1 members, they made numerous contacts with

32

their peers and street people. The field surveillance included night spots and popular hangouts of urban youth. Each investigator kept daily field notes that were reviewed and discussed in weekly meetings. These notes helped develop the questions for later interviews with gang members. By June 1, 1981, the I-Team had sufficient knowledge of the gang to initiate direct contact with the members.

Gang C-1, not a typical youth gang, had several unique characteristics. The code of silence was highly respected and feared by gang members, and the organization was compartmentalized, divided like a large organization or business. These two factors caused investigators a great deal of concern. How complex was the infrastructure?

Gang members spurned I-Team researchers when first approached. When asked if they were gang members, all the subjects responded verbally, ''No,'' projecting a hostile attitude. Since investigators observed what appeared to be drug transactions in broad daylight, they realized that inquiries or confrontation at these street corners, houses, and other places of business could lead to problems of suspicion and confusion by gang members about the intent of our study. Many gang members asked if the investigators were the ''Man,'' ''John Law,'' or the ''Hook''—all meaning police authorities.

Although gang members would not cooperate, many community members gave information, after they were assured that they would not be identified. Merchants, neighbors, and gang-member peers gave their insights and detailed accounts of the gang lifestyle. Two important factors emerged:

1. Younger boys, who were not full members but who worked as surveillance/watch-out persons, talked and even bragged about their work with Gang C-1.

2. Another type of street group or gang emerged during the surveillance and investigations. These gangs were loose-knit, varied in size, and were very different from Gang C-1 in their demeanor. Although they would not make a difference to Detroit (some of these gangs were not even known beyond their own neighborhoods), they provided information about the main gang because they idolized members of Gang C-1.

These gangs, labeled "scavengers" in this study, were numerous in the neighborhood. Two scavenger gangs became secondary subjects. Gang C-1 became so popular that its name and lifestyle were emulated, not only in their own neighborhood, but throughout the metropolitan Detroit area. A suburban upper-middle-class community had a brief problem in 1985 with a corporate gang that united parents and school officials to stop the problem before it grew.

Some of the scavengers auditioned for Gang C-1 acceptance by performing various illegal or criminal acts to prove themselves worthy of membership.

By August 13, 1981, investigators had established contact with several members of two, large scavenger gangs in Detroit (150 and 100 members).* We labeled them Gang S-1 and Gang S-2. Gang S-2 was from the Gang C-1 neighborhood. Gang S-1 was from a nearby neighborhood. Both of these scavenger gangs emulated Gang C-1.

All gangs, corporate or scavenger, revealed a number of similar characteristics.

1. The central purpose of the gang was drug trafficking for enormous profit.

2. Gang members are recruited from various places such as playgrounds, recreation centers, video arcades, schools, and neighborhoods, friends, and associates.

3. Members' jobs ranged from being lookouts to couriers, messengers to distributors, salespersons and crew chiefs to enforcers.

4. Any signs of betrayal to the organization could mean serious consequences and bodily harm.

5. The rewards for working were great—compensation in large amounts of cash, trips to Las Vegas and New York, and exotic, expensive automobiles such as Mercedes Benzes.

6. Gang C-1 was very separate and different. They had professional legal advice on call.

---

*These numbers represent two primary groups or scavenger gang confederacies. Many scavenger members belong to more than one gang.

The investigative team determined that Gang C-1 did make a difference to Detroit. Consequently, our basic premise of Gang C-1's effect on Detroit had been met.

1. It was involved in criminal activities (drugs) that conflicted with the general welfare of the city of Detroit.

2. The gang operated 24 hours a day, particularly in broad daylight, acting as if they had nothing to hide. Professional legal advice was on call.

3. The gang lured teens into membership with promises of attractive materialistic rewards.

4. Gang members became celebrities across the city.

5. Gang C-1, as an organization, competed with traditional employers for manpower.

6. The social impact of gangs on neighborhoods and daily community life was very noticeable.

7. The gang displayed the power to interrupt the educational process as well as the social and family processes of the community.

After reviewing interviews and field notes the research team determined that Gang C-1 was highly organized. Their organization mirrored a big business with corporate style management. The discovery of Gangs S-1 and S-2 established the scavenger type as distinctly separate and different from corporate gangs. The difficult point to put across to Gang C-1 was that this study was for research only. Scavenger gangs were very cooperative after several conversations with investigators.

On September 9, 1981, the investigators agreed with the principal investigator that Gang C-1 was more than an organized youth gang. The street interviews, media reports, gang interviews, and field reports revealed that the gang was earning thousands of dollars daily. Members of the gang wore expensive jewelry and sportswear and drove new high-priced domestic and foreign automobiles. The public showing of their expensive rewards made the gang members kings of this new subculture. The research team labeled them an ''organized corporate type'' gang.

After a year of observation, interviews, and field research, the principal investigator was convinced of the difference that Gang C-1 made in Detroit. Gangs S-1 and S-2 confirmed that groups of youngsters often evolve into possible gangs with no particular purpose—just as they did over fifty years ago. The findings later in this chapter look closely at these two distinct groups. The closer the investigative team looked, the more complex this social phenomenon appeared. The research took a great deal of time to accomplish. Interviews and reviews of relevant materials, individuals, and institutions were conducted from 1980 to 1986.

Corporate gangs represent change; scavenger gangs represent an extension of the past. Gang C-1 is symbolic of urban youth rebellion that has manifested itself into a mutation. It was *the* gang in Detroit. Gang C-1 had a king-of-the-hill reputation. Its city-wide fame caused countless numbers of urban youngsters to emulate it. The most disturbing factor, though, actually extends beyond youth gangs. This study uncovered a new psyche of urban youth that may be nearly impossible to change, control, or even understand. This new psyche or mind-set is self-destructive to the individual as well as devastating to society as a whole.

Over the years, urban youth gangs have seemed to fade away at times, only to reappear and continue their delinquent ways. Unfortunately, corporate gang activities have directly and indirectly caused scavenger gangs to become more violent. Some scavengers, individually and collectively, graduate into corporate type operations. I-Team investigators revealed numerous examples of criminal activities that were never reported. This invisibility of urban youth gang activity and crime results in a grim social dilemma and has exacerbated the destructive mind-set of urban youth. The polarization of blacks and whites underscores the overt hostility growing in the inner city.

Some social scientists contend that America has two societies—the have's and the have-not's. After reviewing the data from this study, the researcher found not only that two societies have emerged but that a third culture exists. This third culture is mixed with underclass and urban gang members who have their own interpretations of American society. After being ignored, impoverished, and poorly educated, this culture exhibits signs of moral erosion and anarchy. America is being tested today in ways much like the early days of the Wild West frontier. Bands of urban youth, some organized and many unorganized and unnamed, are roaming the streets.

COMPLEXITIES OF INVESTIGATION

The problem of interviewing Gang C-1 was very diffi-cult and tedious. Observation of the gang had revealed several important characteristics and idiosyncracies. The breakthrough in penetrating their code of silence came after the gang started to be investigated and indicted by federal authorities. Gang C-1 began to unravel at the seams. Research investigators were then able to move in much closer to younger members, peers, and families because the gang itself was preoccupied with federal investigations and possible indictments. The federal charges caused chaos and confusion as top leaders were investigated and gang members faced the threat of long-term incarceration.

Gang C-1's legal problems produced two important side effects: (1) there was internal bickering over the gang's direction and leadership; and (2) competition arose from outsiders who were trying to take over the lucrative drug business the gang had developed and cultivated.

Street intelligence uncovered other key problems. By November 9, 1981, investigations revealed that Gang C-1 had a competitor. The new gang, Gang C-2, had copied its corporate style. At this point, Gang C-1 reportedly had well over two hundred members and was growing. Investigators found that Gang C-2 had actually been challenging Gang C-1 over the past year, especially along the common border of their territories.

As Gang C-2 emerged, two large scavenger gangs that emulated the corporate-style gangs became very active in the C-1 neighborhood. Investigators were able to capitalize on the admiration and worship the scavengers had for the corporate gangs. Such scavengers were very eager not only to identify with corporate members, but to prove that they were experts on corporate ways and life styles.

Scavengers were easy to approach and interview. They were generally very talkative and some were great braggarts about the feats of their gangs. Corporate members, on the other hand, were silent, unwilling to talk, and very evasive. Prior to indictment, individuals refused to admit that they were gang members, nor did they even acknowledge the existence of the gang. Investigators relied on observations, frequently (daily in some cases) discussing alleged members with the businesses they patronized, social places, sporting events, and schools. Eventually, some corporate members agreed to answer general questions.

One of the safeguards, in addition to violence, that Gang C-1 instituted against members telling gang business was very similar to the Mafia tactic—the ploy of allowing members to know only small amounts of gang business. Like the national crime syndicate, the soldiers in the Mafia don't know who does what at the top. AB, a former gang member now in prison, offered this insight on the ploy:

> You had a job, selling jones. That's your business. . . worrying about anything else could cause you problems. Ask lots of questions, make you seem like the police or something. You don't want to know nothing, but who's paying you for your job. I don't want to know what ain't my concern you see. . . . Being nosey can get you smoked real quick. So long as you getting paid, what else counts?

Roy Hayes, U.S. Attorney for the Eastern District of Michigan, agreed that the ignorance ploy has made pursuit of criminal organizations such as Gang C-1 difficult. The gang was well schooled in using juveniles that were protected by their youthful ages. Hayes said, "Dividing into compartments makes it very difficult to make a strong case when pursuing these types of gangs."

On January 10, 1982, a questionnaire was developed for scavenger gangs and corporate gangs. This was the first of several questionnaires designed for this study. Special consideration was taken when all of the investigators emphasized these problems:

1. Many of the subjects, regardless of category, would under no conditions respond in writing to a questionnaire.

2. Scavengers displayed a high degree of illiteracy and the mere mention of filling out any type of application or questionnaire would jeopardize this or any similar survey.

3. Gang members, corporate types in particular, would become very uncooperative with any mention of names or personal reference that might jeopardize them as informants or leave them vulnerable to law enforcement authorities.

The principal investigator conferred with the police officer/consultant and concluded that in order to preserve the study the investigators needed to follow these guidelines:

1. Guarantee (or at least make a strong promise) the subjects that no names would be recorded or used. This included nicknames which often identified individuals in gangs better than their birth names.

2. Guarantee that this study was for research to understand urban youth gangs only. As researchers, we had no other motives. However, if they were worried about our intent, they should refrain from giving any information they considered critical or possibly damaging since our study would be released for public information.

3. Give the subjects a 24-hour, seven-days-a-week, phone number to use in the event that they had any questions.

4. Guarantee all subjects that no hidden tape recorders would be used. Investigators would inform subjects that interviews would be taped. If subjects objected, the investigator would not use the tape recorder.

5. Guarantee that all conversations and interviews were confidential. (We emphasized guideline #2). Investigators promised under no circumstances to name sources to other gangs or internally to fellow gang members.

The guidelines were instrumental in gaining the confidence of gang members. Although scavengers were much easier to communicate with, they regarded questions as authoritarian. The key to asking questions was sincerity on the part of the investigators. This point was reiterated by the principal investigator. The principal investigator and the chief field investigator relied on past contacts with gangs at major events at Cobo Hall and Joe Louis Arena. The police officer/consultant proved most valuable with his keen insight on urban crime and inner-city youngsters. The study involved countless hours of verbal exchange, observation, and interaction in gang hangouts, on neighborhood streets, and at sporting events.

After several meetings with the consultant and the investigative team, it was decided that there would be both group interviews and individual interviews. The group interviews were held in various places throughout the city. The rationale for groups was that this would allow the gang members to relax, see other members discuss questions, and mainly, to introduce our method of reading the questions and writing their answers down on paper. The group sessions were freely and spontaneously conducted. They had a feeling of closeness much like that of a locker-room or bull session. Investigators worked in teams of two: one asked set questions from a printed questionnaire and wrote down the group's responses. The other interviewer observed and recorded any additional comments members might add to the subject.

The population for this study was drawn from corporate gangs C-1 and C-2 and scavenger gangs S-1, S-2, S-3, and S-4. Group size varied at interviews but was never greater than ten at one time. The verbal method relaxed the scavengers because many resented subjects such as writing and reading in school.

The investigators dressed casually. Many investigators carried recorder-radio units to many interviews. They selected currently popular music to play on their "ghetto blasters." This music was helpful in creating an easy, relaxed atmosphere. The music was played at low levels. Gang members enjoyed the music and often responded positively to the questions. Although field investigators had questioned gang members before, this was the first attempt to collect data for specific categorical questions. The pretest and field surveys helped shape the questions for the group session and individual sessions. Group interviews were begun on January 17, 1982.

The group interviews assisted the team in developing additional, individual questions for the two gang types. Interviews were prearranged by investigators. The understanding and use of street lingo, language, and specific terminologies gave investigators credibility with gang members.

The survey focused on both corporate-style and scavenger gangs. Forty individuals from each gang type were chosen for the individual sessions. The group sessions had twenty corporate members and twenty scavenger gang members. Other interviews were with community members, who were chosen in the field during neighborhood investigations. For example, investigators had learned from street sources that CD, 16 years old and a member of Gang C-2, had recently purchased a brand-new BMW 733. Although CD wouldn't talk, investigators met a group of ten-year olds who called themselves the Baby C-2s. This group of young-sters described some of the inner workings of the gang as if they were charter members. Two years later some of the Baby C-2s had graduated into the gang. Since investigators had an ongoing relationship with the former Baby members, a new direct line had been established.

Examples such as these were numerous and arose while canvassing gang neighborhoods. Many community members were willing to talk off the record. Many times, inside information on gangs came from family members. Surprisingly, some members were bragging about a relative gang member's success in the group while others were disgusted with his membership in these gangs. The data from outside sources in these neighborhoods, business transactions, and playgrounds were invaluable.

While surveying the neighborhood of Gang C-1, the investi-gators discovered several groups of black males ranging from ages 11 to 17. These groups were constantly changing in size and leadership. (Yablonsky's description of near-groups fits these youngsters in a general sense.) The uniqueness of these neighborhood groups is that they would join a "confederacy" of a sort with other neighborhood groups and grow into a new type of urban gang, the scavengers. Many of the young boys in the Gang C-1 neighborhood and adjoining neighborhoods glorified Gang C-1. Despite the fact that scavengers had no set goals or purposes, they all had one bonding point. They all knew about corporate gangs. The near-groups came from similar backgrounds that the traditional Detroit street groups evolved from over the past fifty years.

It was very difficult to interview the urban residents of Detroit. Citizens who lived in neighborhoods with gangs were very hesitant to talk. Without street experience and keen insight, the investigative team would have been unable to obtain any interviews. The advantage of knowing the families of some of gang members, their peers, and their neighborhoods, was valuable. Members of corporate type gangs, particularly, conducted their business and affairs by something like the Mafia's code of "omerta."*

Many inner-city black youth in Detroit are bilingual, but most speak only street language. This language is black English, mixed with local fad and hip-hop (rap) lingo. The investigators were also bilingual and understood this fast-paced form of communication. In the following interviews, obtained over a five-year period, participants are identified only by generic first names. For example, "John, age 16, said, . . ." All other names have been changed to protect the subjects.

These interviews contain some cursing as well as vulgar and explicit street language. To tamper with or remove any of this language would have robbed this study of meaningful content and accuracy.

---

*Code of Silence—talk to no one outside the organization.

The choice of subjects for interviews resulted from dialogues with various individuals in Detroit. Actual names of gangs, individuals, or nicknames, have not been used at any time in any part of this study.

SUBJECT: THE AUTO INDUSTRY

The subject of working in Detroit was discussed by the interviewer with six members of a scavenger gang. The question was asked, *Wouldn't the members of your gang rather work at an auto plant such as Chrysler?*

Rodney, 16 years old, laughed:

> Hell, no . . . the plant is for suckers. My cousin Darren worked at Fords and he thought it was happening. He worked all day, overtime, all the time for peanut money. Now my boy Jerome he's younger than Darren and he already got two brand new rides. He works when he wants and he's making big money. Factory money ain't no money. Jerome is rolling with the T's. He used to be with us, but he hooked up with Howard at school and got lucky and joined the T's. When you're rolling, life is sweet . . . you can buy anything and folks respect you. Darren told me that I could deliver pizza or work at Wendy's [laughing loudly]. Right! for three or four dollars! No way, work your ass to death and you got nothing. Anyway, the plant got lame-ass foremen, some black and some white, telling dudes like me to do this and assign them the worst jobs. . . . Ain't nobody telling me shit.
>
> That's why our crew is my thing. I do what I want. When you get with a crew everything works. If you get with the real fellas like Jerome did, then you get paid like big time action. The T's drive Benzo's, 'vettes, Renegades, got big paper and all the bitches they want. Now ain't no factory boys catching that all star action, like the T's. If you work in the plant you're making dough for that ass Lee Iacocca. Work eight hours a day is for suckers. Our crew finds something to make doughski. We don't want no bullshit factory jobs, we want rolling money. . . . Me and my homeboys just waiting to get with the T's or W's so we can get paid in full.

Doug, 15 years old; Joe, 14 years old; Benny, 17 years old. (These participants discussed the subject of factory jobs.)

Joe:

My sister's boyfriend works at Buick up in Flint and he acts like the job is his wife. Later for all that work hard crap. Me and Doug, we gonna be rappers.

Doug:

Fuck that factory rap, we going to sell some dope and get paid. Then we'll go into the studio and make our rap record and be stars. . . . All I want to do is get paid and show all them suckers at school that school ain't shit. Me and the boys getting paid and we ain't wasting our time doing no lame-ass factory gig.

Benny:

Me, I got it made, I got a woman who got a rough apartment, get food stamps. The crew get paid, so why should I work in some old dirty noisy car factory? I work out at the spa, pump iron and play basketball up at the rec league. The niggahs in the plant started to bug when they started closing plants in the city. So who needs a job, when all you got to do is get with a crew that's rolling? . . . You can make a month's pay in a little more than a week. Me, I got it all worked out, later for all that school, job, marrying shit. . . . Just get me some paper.

SUBJECT: SELLING DRUGS

The interviewer asked Louis, aged 14 and member of a corporate gang: *Don't you know that selling drugs is illegal and morally wrong?*

Louis replied:

Wrong? What's wrong? Look . . . [sigh] I'm doing what people want, what's wrong about giving people what they want? I ain't using the shit, I just sell drugs. I'm just selling suckers what they

45

need. If they want and I got it, why not! People get high all over the world and anyway everybody getting high . . . what's illegal? Man, you would be surprised at who cops dope from us. If people didn't want dope, we couldn't sell it, but people want dope. Illegal, says who? Look at all the drunks, drinking used to be illegal. I heard my Uncle Bru talk about when you couldn't get no whiskey, the bullshit white man always talking that yang . . . the same shit talking people cop my bags to get high. . . . Cigarettes should be illegal. They kill lots of stupid mutha-fuckas, but the rich-ass white man selling tons of squares, smoking bunches of dumb-ass people right to hell, so what's illegal? Everything is illegal, let all the hammerhead squares tell you. . . . Like some teachers at the school, they talk about be good and study. Them same dudes be trying to get with the cuties, know what I mean? Everybody want some sex, cash and dope . . . teachers, preachers, big time business people, ball players, the whole damn world gets high. . . . Anyway, where you think all the dope come from? Me and my crew just selling the shit like all the other crews round the world. I use to go out with this cutie, and her momma cracked on me and my boys for some paper and dope. . . . She said the dope was for her man. I gave her some bags and now she calls me all the time begging for deals on coke and can she get credit. I stopped seeing the daughter 'cause she was bugging the shit out of me for dope all the time. Oh, oh, yeah, she worked for the gas company and she tried to front like she was a church woman, but I know a fiend when I see one and she was out cold.

Now me, I don't fuck with no dope, I save my money. . . . If people knew how much cash I got, they would be trying to get next to me. I ain't telling you all how much, so don't even think about it [smiling]. If I wasn't rolling I'd be poor, with no cash, but I'm set, got plenty of clothes, cash and bitches. When I get sixteen, I'm going to cop me a brand ride. Ain't decided but you can bet it's going to be sweet. Right now, I rent me a limo, or ride with my boys, half of them got fresh rides. . . . Selling dope is just business, my peoples don't talk about it. I don't flash my shit, I give my peoples money. I'm still learning how to roll, now in about a year I'll be rolling hard. If you be cool and roll without making lots of yang yang, you'll get paid big. The way I see it rolling is the only way a fella can make it today. . . .

Scavenger gang members were asked why the crew sells drugs.

Junior, age 16, explained:

> It's a way to get over. Selling jones is the way to make it today. . . . We don't give a damn about legal. What's legal anyway? Me and my homeboys want to hook up with the Roes. You need status and cash to get ahead. If we were getting paid like the Roes, we be straight. Selling dope ain't no different than selling cars or houses. Anyway, I don't give a fuck about nobody. . . . I don't care about nobody. Me and my crew if we can't sell no dope, we going to find something to beast on . . . . Ain't no jobs, so we may as well beast or steal. That's just the way it be. . . . Sooner or later our crew will be running the shit over in this side of the town.

Darly, age 15, another member of Junior's crew, continued on the subject of selling drugs:

> It's like this, if we don't sell the shit, somebody else will. Niggahs getting paid in full, slinging dope hard every day. So why should we take some bullshit ass minimum wage McDonalds' job? Fuck, everything is illegal [laughing]. Pork is deadly, bacon can kill niggahs, whiskey, cigarettes, cars, guns, but ain't nobody stopping them companies from selling them!

Larry, 15, interrupted:

> The rollers only arrest us, the young niggahs, they don't fuck with the rich mugs that sell dope. My brother went to Vietnam and he said the government let Viet Nam dudes bring big dope from Nam. My brother got his head all jammed in that war over there. Legal or illegal, I don't care, I want to get paid. . . . People will play you and trick your ass. Me, I ain't getting tricked by nobody.

SUBJECT: ROLE MODELS IN AMERICA

The interviewer told Raymond, 13 and a scavenger, that ministers, teachers, lawyers, and doctors are successful and positive role models in the community. Raymond protested:

Positive? You must be ill. . . . All them niggahs is fraudulent. . . . They be perpetrators, they ain't real. I know plenty of them kind of niggahs that get high and love some young tender ronies. They be trying to bone them and plenty of them big time niggahs be buying dope and illing all the time. I know this preacher at my momma's church, he ain't shit. How come he gets to wear lots of gold chains, watches, and rings? The congregation ain't nothing but his hos. He lives in some big old house, they pay for everything, plus he get a brand new Lincoln every year. My cousin Ron, he's with the [C-1], and he's getting paid. He gave his momma a new Riviera and plenty of paper. She belong to the same church my momma. The preacher wouldn't look her way when she was poor, but now she getting paid and the dirty ass no good preacher trying to long-dick my aunt and momma. That role model shit is phony and fraudulent. Teachers, preachers, policemen, firemen, lawyers, dentists, everybody is fucking around with dope. We know some fraudulent niggahs talking on television and radio about saying NO, and you see them at parties getting fucked up. I ain't naming no names, not now. Let them sweat and worry if we going to blow their mouth pieces out [laughing]. The only role model we need is George Washington, Thomas Jefferson, Abe Lincoln, and rest of the dead presidents on some hard green cash backs. If I can't spend it, fuck it. I don't need or want it. . . .

Willie, 14 and another scavenger, described his ideal role model to the interviewer.

Tony Montana in 'Scarface' and Lee Iacocca, now they be gangster-down. Scarface had the big dope, big money . . . def bitches, def guns, rough rides, he was fucking mugs up. Lee Iacocca is smooth and he be dissing everybody. . . . He lives like it ain't shit. Lee be sharp in his suits and he's getting paid. That's why I don't want to be in no factory, Lee getting paid while all the dumb, lame-ass mugs getting dirty and losing benefits and cash. I heard my mother's boyfriend talking about how Lee was getting millions while the dumb-ass workers was getting fucked right up their asses!

SUBJECT: MARRIAGE

This interview was the result of an argument between some scavenger gang members regarding the subject of marriage.

Hank 18, had gotten a girl pregnant and was considering marriage. Lee, 14, offered Hank his advice that marriage is "stupid." Hank reflected on his situation:

> *I could get a real job maybe, getting married to Debbie would be OK, she gets a word processing job when she graduates from the business academy next month. This crew shit ain't paying much. . . . Deb's cool people, we could get a apartment and just chill for awhile. Anyway, Lee, what do you know about getting married or babies?*

Lee screamed at Hank:

> *Sucker. I know that marriage is for suckers, later for that bitch, let her have the baby. You ain't got to marry nobody 'cause they going to have a baby. What's a baby? If I get a bitch pregnant she can go have it or whatever else she want, 'cause the kid don't give a shit. . . . The crew is going to be def real soon and you stupid-ass going to be changing diapers full of piss and shit! Fuck the bitch, let her have the damn baby. . . . Look at me, didn't nobody care about me when I was a baby and I came out cool, so what's the big deal? How you going to get a job, you ain't finish school, you can't do nothing but steal and sell dope, fool.*

Marvin, 17, another member of Lee and Hank's gang, interjected his feelings regarding babies.

> *Babies ain't no big thing. I got four kids by different babes. Lee is right, you ain't got to marry no babe just because she's having your baby. Me, I don't do nothing for mine. I figure like this, didn't nobody give a damn bout me and I made it so they'll be OK, just like me. One of the babes I got fat had her brother and*

mother talking that marriage stuff. I just looked at them and laughed. . . . Right, get married and be like my man Bill Cosby with the def kids [laughing]. I'm a terrorist, a gangster, I don't want no family, the fellas, they my family. . . . I don't want no babe and I ain't got no time for no marriage life. What you going to get married for? I see all the players and they ain't married. If you know a bitch, why marry her? You already got her. . . . Marriage is for fools, you can shack up, but who needs marriage? When you tired of a bitch fuck her and kick her ass to the curb. . . . That is what my old man did to my momma. . . .

SUBJECT: SPORTS

The interviewer asked William, 15; Jerry, 16; Clarence, 18; and Darwin, 14, from a corporate gang, how they felt about sports and sport celebrities. William started the conversation.

I like baseball and basketball. When we get time, I go to see the Pistons and Tigers. Rolling lets you make cash so you can go see the games. My uncle talks about when the Pistons used to play at Cobo Arena. Now you got to drive out to Pontiac, it would be sweet if they played downtown . . . . Ball players get paid swell, but it takes too much work to try and make that kind of money. I just play ball for fun, and roll and get paid. Our crew goes to all the games and big fights. Sometimes if your crew been taking care shit, the big fellas will give them tickets to the Tigers. I likes Gibson, Sweet Lou Whitaker and the beastmaster Parrish. I wish they would change their uniforms. That stiff ass big D looks real funny. They need some new hip uniforms.

Jerry and Clarence concurred with William:

The bitches being scoping on us at the Pistons. We be looking so clever that they be jumping up and down begging for us to check them out. Me and Clarence don't go to the Tigers 'cause ain't no bitches at baseball games. Our crew is like a team. . . . We play basketball in the rec league. We got some pro outfits; some of the fellas are from the neighborhood. They don't belong to the crew, but they can jam on the court so we pay them to play. Couple of them used to play college ball. Our boys be beasting when we play. The big fellas be betting on the games. Sometimes the gym be packed with bitches, and the parking lot look like Benzo city. . . . Our crew is celebrities, lots of the pro boys party at our functions and everybody be getting tore down on that caine, even pro boys from outta town.

Clarence interrupted loudly:

Everybody but the ugly-ass Celtics with punk-ass Larry Bird. We hate the punk-ass Celtics and that big nose, ugly Larry Bird. He ain't nothing but a little bitch, crying. If we could play the Celtics, we slam dunk all them green and white suckers. They perpetrators, they's hos, the niggahs that play for the Celtics need to be beasted on. Isaiah, Vinnie, all the Pistons, if they asked us, we pop all them faggot-ass fraudulent Celtics.

SUBJECT: PRISONS AND DETENTION HOMES

Nine male scavengers, ranging in age from 14 to 19, were asked if they were concerned about going to prison.

Donnie responded:

The joint? Scared, worried about jail? No way, not the kid. . . . The youth home is really down. If you get sent to the youth home it ain't no big thing. . . I ain't been to the big time, but when I do, it'll be cool. Everybody I know been to Jack house, three of my boys doing a bit now. . . . Going away is just part of being out here. The youth home people is cool. Some niggahs be clowning, trying to cause shit, they be beasting on folks for nothing, but that's whacked out and causes you more problems. If you be cool and straight, they let you be cool. Some jokers try to fuck with you, I mean the workers at the home. Sometimes it be a whitey and sometimes it be a blood trying to make you into some little fag. I let them know that Donnie ain't no ho. If I get a hard headed worker, I just chill out and don't say a word. Let them do all the talking and wolfing. I just stare at them. . . . If they try getting tough, putting their hands on me, then I start beasting back. They know what's up. Most of the time you know everybody in the home so it's like being with your crew inside. If there's somebody you don't like or know then it's OK to fuck with them, or fuck them like a woman [laughing].

Pete continued:

> The big time is just there like the streets. You got your punks, beastmasters, faggots and some clever dudes all staying together. Sometimes the prison people don't even know that the crew from the streets is down inside. My brothers are inside Jack town and they say the joint just like the street. The guards be fucking with you sometimes, but if you know what's up you lay low, and say later for their stiff asses. The guards ain't like the hook out in the streets. Some dudes belong to the muslims, some go with their homeboys and some just chill out and don't get with nobody. You can get dope and anything else you want in the joint.

James, recently released from a half-way house, explained:

> Pussy, money, food: you want it? You could get anything if you had the paper. I got out on the release program—I just chilled when the guards watched me. A lot of dudes like prison because it's where all their boys is.

Sam and Jason expressed their views of prison life:

> Everybody is talking about John Smith, the enforcer for the Roes. He's at Jackson, living the life. He hooked up with old gangster Joe Doe, and works inside for him. John told my brothers that he's learning more gangster stuff from Joe Doe. He's eating good and he got a young white boy that they done turned out and he's his little pussy bitch. I heard he/she is blond and fine. John pumps iron all day and looks like Conan. He's getting paid by Joe Doe for beasting on folks that owe Joe Doe money. Joe Doe can get anything you want in prison. Doe was the man back in 1974. . . . Prison life can get a fella straight if he hook up with the right people.

Scott, 14, from a corporate gang, has a different view of prisons:

> Prison is for mugs that make mistakes. My crew don't make many mistakes. I ain't ever been stopped by no rollers. What I do is lay low and be cool. Going to prison don't scare me 'cause I know I ain't going. I'm too young for prison first of all, and second, I ain't

even been near the detention home, unless one of my partners is getting out. If you know what you are doing, you can't get caught. The crews that get live and flashy are asking for trouble. Not me, I like being free and smooth. Prison is for clowns who can't handle the life. Me, I'm cool. I ain't going nowhere.

SUBJECT: SCHOOL, HIGHER EDUCATION

The interviewer asked some members of a corporate gang, ages 12 to 14, how they felt about going to school and their future educational plans. Russell led the response:

School is OK. You can have a slick time at school. I like school and everybody knows we're down so it's kind of like we're the stars . . . the cuties want to get with you, 'cause you're rolling and they know you getting paid. I get to wear my slick shit, and everybody checks you out. I like the cuties, the clothes. Learning about math and science ain't bad really. I like my counselor and some of my teachers. I think my counselor knows about me and the crew.

Phillip and Herman intervened:

Lot of jit niggahs trying to get with us. They want to hook up with us, 'cause they know the bitches want our crew. We're the shit at school and in our neighborhood. It's us the stars. Jit boys try to dress like us [laughing], but they can't buy no rolling clothes with general assistance paper. . . . The Noe Crew, they be begging like little women, trying to get close to us. They be talking trash about what they done did . . . they done popped this niggah and they done did this [laughing]. Everybody at our school want to join the fellas. . . .

Bobby reflected on his reasons for not liking school:

I hate school, I'm trying to sell my bags at school. Teachers, counselors, all of them be dissing people. I can remember getting dissed by teacher when I first started school. . . . Later for school, I like getting neat, wearing my outfits, having cash and driving my scooter around the schoolyard . . . make the big foot security dude real mad. School is where I meet people and sell my bags. I sell to anybody, lots of dope fiends at school and they all ain't young students [laughing].

53

Malcolm seriously revealed his future plans:

I'm going to college, I'm getting good grades now and I know what's happening. . . . Now, you check out the crazy jit niggahs in the Noes, they out cold. They going to be illing, crying on welfare. But our crew will be cruising 'cause we getting paid. I'm going to become a lawyer. Lawyers dress good and they make straight cash. Now, most of these boys ain't going to college but they ain't fucking up like the Noes. Most niggahs ain't thinking about the future. . . . Me and my boys saving our paper and gonna get us a real business. We got a lawyer who's down, he's getting paid by us. Lawyers tell you up front, 'I can't take your case until you put up $5,000 cash. . . .' See they getting paid right up front, all cash, so that's why I want to be a lawyer. I got plenty of brains. I don't like that rough stuff, that gangster killing shit, that ain't me. I just want to get paid. College life is all prep and I like the prep style. It's real down. . . . College cuties is happening and they like paper and hip rides. If you go to college, you drive one of those little sport cars and dress preppy. Now the Noes and the Moes they ain't going nowhere. . . . But me, I'll become a lawyer and represent crews and tell them how to stay fresh and clever. . . .

Bobby insisted that college wasn't for him:

Everybody I know at college acts like they different from us. Bloods go to college and they try to act special. They walk different, talk different—try to act white. College niggahs be talking preppy and dissing bloods, but they ain't got no paper, they fake, fraudulent . . . they niggahs but they try to act like they like whities at college. Why go to school or college? Outside of selling my bags, college ain't shit to me. I know plenty of preppy dope heads. Freaks that graduated from college and they are now here begging and fronting. Lots of them would be rolling if they had the balls to get out here. Preppy college boys be fronting like they gangsters, but they fake. My sister used to go to college. She went out with college boys. She found out that they ain't got no paper, they be poor, they be fronting, talking about lunch and big business deals. My sister and her girls found out quick, that college boys talk white and want to be rolling like my crew. Now my sister and her girls done got with the program and they with some crew fellas and they fresh and rolling. . . . Hey, yo-yo, did you go to college, man? [asking the interviewer].

54

Is that why you asking all these def questions about our stuff, like rolling and beasting?

Dickie:

That is ho work, college preps be illing tough. Have you seen how they dress? Raggedy clothes, torn-up blue jeans, ugly-ass sweatshirts, bullshit glasses. College is for suckers and hos, they ain't getting paid. I know plenty of deadheads that been to college and they out cold. Plus, after you finish they ain't making no paper. Half of them college boys be trying to act white. They talk funny, like white boys, and they don't want nobody from the hood to speak to them.

On the subject of working, Dickie reacted:

Work in a plant? Are you ill? Plants be noisy, dirty, and have mugs screaming bullshit orders—and they pay ho-wages. That money ain't shit compared to rolling. I'm going to roll until I leave here. My momma talk about how proud she is of me making doughski. She used to dog me and say I wasn't shit, but now she's proud. See, when you getting paid, everybody, I mean everybody, want to get with you. My grandfather worked in the plant for thirty years. Now he always disses my momma, brothers, and me. I took my boy Freddy by his house to let my grandfather see the mobile home Freddy bought his people. Now my grand builted a camper for his truck—it's slick but it ain't shit compared to Freddy's mobile home. Granddaddy won't let no women on his camper. Reason is that he got naked pictures of all kinda women over the walls. The old man is crazy about naked women. He's always preaching about school and church, but I know he's a freak all the way. Anyway, Granddaddy treats Freddy with respect now, and he don't dis me no more. I think he's confused. If he knew where the paper was coming from, he probably freak out.

SUBJECT: VIOLENCE

Clarence, a corporate, was asked how violence affects him.

Violence is messy, I don't like it. The violence in crew business is necessary, it's just part of business. Now jits like the [S-1], they like violence: beating, messing with any and everybody that

55

causes problems for our crew. I ain't talking about our enforcers, I could come up stinking. Lot of times it's Zero action, you know? Zeroes* like to beast on anybody. We got some Zeroes on our demolition crew** but I stay clear of them. Zeroes don't care about nothing. They ain't afraid to die over any stupid thing. At least our Zeroes work a niggah cause, the crew say do it. But the Noes got some whacked Zeroes. They like to rape babes, beat up people and kill somebody for fun. There's a lot of dudes stanking and it ain't nothing but some zero action. Me, I rather chill—take it slow and get me a babe and listen to some sounds.

Now if somebody catch trouble with our beastmasters it's about paper usually. Doughski makes people ill, you know? If somebody messes with your property, then they need to be checked. I don't call that violence, that's just tightening your business up. Mostly, I just count my paper and let the knuckle boys wreck fake people. Every time somebody gets bloody I get real sick to my stomach. Big Paul dogs me because I can't stand bloody things. But them crazy-ass demo-boys like to hurt niggahs. They just like to beast on whoever's around. Our crew enforces when people ill on them. But I think some of them boys would beast on somebody for free. That is why I stay clear of them. They dangerous if you get on their bad side.

O'Dell, a scavenger, 18, described his thinking regarding violence:

I likes to bust heads. Violence? What's that? [laughing] You got to dog everybody or they gonna dog you. Doggin' is my specialty. I'm the dog-master. I dogs men, boys, girls, bitches, my momma, teachers, policemen, policebitches, my momma's boyfriends. I'll just see somebody and start doggin' them in the street.

Me and my boys like to crush mugs and kick ass at school, in the bathrooms, gym or lockerroom. The [S-4] tried to dog us at a house party last month. I got so pissed that I got me a Uzi from my cousin (he's in the [C-2]), and went to one of the [S-4] house and sprayed that sucker. After that, when the [S-4] see me and the crew, they leave real quick. I got put out of school for beasting on this teacher. This big, ugly security guard tried to stop me from kicking the teacher's ass. It took four guards to stop me from killing that bitch. They put me

---

*zero mentality—a person who does not care about anything; has nothing to lose; capable of anything at any time.
**Not actual name

in the youth home: big, fucking deal. They called my old man. He said they could keep me. FU-CK him, he ain't shit, he's a crackhead just like my ho-assed mammy. My old man let me live with him when I was eight or nine years old. He used to beat the shit out of me until I got big and started kicking his ass. Him and my momma dog each other all the time. Both of them dog me and my brothers real bad. When my momma would start illing she get my clothes and throw them out the front door. I hated that! Then my old man wouldn't help me with nothing, including getting something to eat. So, I just said fu-ck everybody and everything. I love to jump on preppies, punk-ass dudes, or preppy hos, it don't matter. If I see somebody with gold or whatever, they better check it in real quick. I likes seeing little scared preppies when we beast on their asses. My crew is the beasting crew—crushing asses is our way of having fun.

SUBJECT: TRAINING PROGRAMS, JOB MARKET

The interviewer asked Rafael, 19, *What are the chances for you taking up a legal job or getting into a program that will train you for a better paying job?*

Rafael answered:

Better paying jobs ain't in this world for bloods, especially young bloods. I been kicking it with a crew since I was thirteen. I ain't telling y'all where, but I got my paper stashed and I'm still rolling. Some of the fellas after that got busted, had to join job training fake-ass programs. Train you for what? A cook? Bullshit janitor job? A security guard that pays $3.65 an hour? Or maybe one of those good paying skilled jobs like welding. Yeah . . . welding, that's what my brother did at Dodge Main until they layed him off, after fourteen and a half years. . . they said, "We'll retrain you." Right! Yo, he already has a skill! They gave my brother some paper for his time in and told him to go to the re-training cen-ter. . . . He went and some preppy bitch dissed him, the bitch acted like she was better than him. Made him feel real bad, make him feel like he was begging, groveling for her black bitch ass working for the lying-ass whities. I told him Fu-ck that perpetrating fake-ass bitch. So he took his money and got with me and my crew and now he's rolling. We got some straight legal shit. Can't tell y'all 'cause the hook always trying to dog.

> *My brother's partner lost his job and went through that train-*
> *ing shit. They fucked him over real good. . . . Now he just drink*
> *beer, whiskey, or smoke joints and borrow money from my*
> *brother. His bitch splitted with his kids. When you ain't got*
> *no cash, nobody respects you. Bloods ain't got no future in*
> *no job market. I've been rolling, making paper, and laying low.*
> *My brother is rolling and he's cool.*
>
> *Now my daddy worked in the plant thirty-three years. He put*
> *me out because I was with the fellas. Him and my momma was*
> *big drugged at me for hooking up with the crew. But later for all*
> *that college and good job shit. I got two other older brothers and*
> *one sister. My sister went to college and graduated. My daddy*
> *was real proud of her. She married this prep boy. Now they got*
> *a little bullshit apartment, a stiff ass compact car and their jobs*
> *ain't shit. My sister she act like I'm some gangster. She's illing*
> *all the time. They always borrowing paper from my people. My*
> *daddy talk about how well and good they doing, but he got*
> *to loan them money every month [laughing]. My other brother*
> *went to the war, you know, Viet Nam. He married some oriental*
> *bitch and they never come back to the city. He went to college,*
> *and now he's a manager of some fake-ass hotel in Arizona. My*
> *daddy act like he don't know how my brother that's rolling is*
> *getting paid. He know, but he don't want to let me know that*
> *it's cool. But a fella ain't got no choice. It's roll or get rolled by*
> *all the perpetrators out here. My sister dissed me and my brother*
> *one Sunday over our place. She's preaching and calling us dope*
> *pushers, gangsters and all kinds of nasty names. I got tired and*
> *I just checked her. I told her, "Look who buys our bags. Everybody*
> *and bunches of whities in big cars, little fancy sport cars. Caine is*
> *what everybody is doing. Anyway, if your punk-ass husband was*
> *really smart, he know that the government got Ollie North selling*
> *CONTRA-Cocaine all over the world!"*

SUBJECT: FEMALES IN GANGS

The interviewer asked a group of female corporate gang members why they were joining or forming groups. Brenda, 15; Carol, 16; Diane, 15; Lisa, 13; and Mary, 16, responded.

Brenda:

> *Girls throw just like guys. We want paper and respect like the*
> *fellas. All of us were friends and went to school and hung out*
> *after school. Me and Lisa are cousins. Diane and Carol live down*

the street from me. My man is in the [C-2] and was asking me to do this and that for him. Sometimes he paid good and sometimes he pay me like I was a ho, paying me ho money.

Lisa and her boyfriend started making paper 'cause he was in the crew with my man. Carol used to drive my man's car whenever I needed to go somewhere and I didn't have no license. Now I drive 'cause we got some fake licenses, but usually Carol drives. So, anyway, we were getting paper off and on for little favors and jobs. You know, first everybody on the block was freaking 'cause we were with the [C-2], next we was driving big cars and dressing fresh. It was fun, big fun, it was live. After doing favors, Carol and Diane started talking about us making paper like the fellas. We were already working like some of the crew guys. Chuckie showed us how to shoot a Mac 10, Uzi, and one 'em was a .357 Magnum. After a while we started seeing all kind of girl crews at parties, basketball games, and at the Lady (a night club).

Carol continued:

Everybody started calling us the [C-2]-ettes at school and in the hood. People knew not to fuck with us 'cause of the fellas.

Lisa interrupted:

Yo, some bonehead niggahs trying to bum rush a party we gave. They was some rinkey dink crew called the Two's (scavenger gang, small, unknown). They thought they could beast on us 'cause we were girls."

Diane proclaimed victory:

"Yeah, until I cut loose on their fake asses with that Uzi. Everybody found out that night that some tramp-ass crew don't mean shit to us. Our crew is just like the fellas. We joined the crew to make paper just like fellas. OK? If we can work for the crew, why can't we be a crew?

The interviewer asked the group, *Do you ever date or social- ize with non-gang males?*

Rene answers:

If a guy ain't got no crew, he probably ain't got no cash. Guys with no paper don't interest us. If you ain't got no paper, what do I need you for?

Angela laughed and added:

This boy at my school wants to get with me. He's cute, plays on the basketball team at school. I could get with him. I told him that I could get him with the Woes. He got real ill, started acting nervous and stopped talking with me. I asked him, "What's up, Baby?" He said he didn't know I was down with the crew action. This fool told me he had a job at the gas station. I said, "Look here, fella, how you going to get with me and you ain't got no paper?" He was drugged. We just laughed. Fuck them. Got no cash, got no time.

Others complained:

Crew guys have stupid paper. It's serious with crew fellas.

Andrea said:

My momma likes Michael 'cause he brings her real nice gifts. Now some boy working at Mickey Dee's ain't got no gift paper, you know?

Deborah agrees:

I want nice things. I likes BMWs, Volvos and Benzos. Some niggah tried rapping to me, talking about going out on a date, taking the bus . . . I said, "Niggah, please!"

Lynn lectured:

Check it. Crews got paper, rides and def clothes. My sister used to get with older fellas and try to get paid. She told me, "Get it all, Baby, get it all." So that's why we got our own thing. We get paid for being the Woes women and then we get paid for being a crew. It's too sweet.

GANG LIFE

The subculture of gang life in Detroit revealed various attitudes. Current gang members, former members, families of members, and non-gang members differed on the subject of gang life. Scavenger gangs displayed the traditional patterns of troubled youth, yet, their propensity to castigate violence against society seems to have escalated in recent years. The following interviews describe a wrestling of the traditional behavior of scavengers with the new age of youth gangs. Gangsterism has had a profound effect on inner city youth. Interestingly, this impact is reported from both pro and con perspectives.

The corporate-style youth gangs have embraced a culture of materialism. The socioeconomics of organized youth gangs separates them not only from scavenger types but also from families, friends, and society. Corporate gangs deliver a one-two punch to inner city youth. First, the image of corporate members is stating, "This is it, this is the *organization to belong to. . . .*" Secondly, the impression has visible hard-core evidence that crime pays, and pays well. The field interviews outline opposing views on whether gang life is positive or negative for its participants.

SUBJECT: ARE GANGS WORTH TRYING?

Larry, 17, a former scavenger gang member, commented:

I got put away for trying to flip a little caine. If I had been with the [C-2], this bullshit wouldn't happened. Crews with connects and paper, they down. If you be rolling hard, a crew is the only way. Now I'm in some bullshit training program that pays $3.75 an hour . . . supposed to be learning about making houses, paying me some welfare dough. I'm on probation, got some white boy counselor, who's illing talking about my family and how good this program be. Well, if it's so good, how come they paying bullshit money? I got to get paid, the crew action is the only gig I need. Now after this training shit you think somebody going to let me make them a house? Right, the bloods ain't getting paid this kind of doughski to make houses. The fat ass teacher and the little fake counselors getting more paper than $3.75 an hour. This program is ripping me off 'cause I got caught trying to sling some caine . . . now my old crew didn't have the big-time lawyers. I got a partner who knows some boys in the Woes and we going to get hooked up and get paid. Man, the crew is worth everything, it's the shit. You think I'm going to work for $3.75 an hour? Soon as I get rid of this dick-head probation officer I'm back with some crew.

SUBJECT: IMPACT OF GANGS ON FAMILIES

Denise, 21, spoke about her brother Dennis, 16, a member of a corporate gang:

My brother has become different in the past two years. My family used to be real tight, you know? Dennis was doing good at school. He started wanting to talk to some girl whose brother was rolling. My mother works afternoons so we always had to stay over my grand's after school, she lives next door to our house. My two little brothers used to look up to Dennis . . . last year he started wearing expensive jewelry, I mean big ugly chains, and talking all that rap crap.

My mother and him started arguing all the time. He started talking back to my grand and momma. He hadn't never did no crazy talk before. My momma don't play—she told him he better get right or she put him out. I'm going to college and I got a little job at the campus book store. Dennis used to talk about going to college and playing basketball. All he used to talk about was Michael Jordan and Magic Johnson. Dennis used to play basketball every day, even on Sundays. He used to belong to the youth choir at church and he used to do anything for my grand or Uncle William. He started going out with that dope girl and he just changed overnight. First, he stay away from home for two, three days. My mother would call the police, but they couldn't help. Next, he started driving that girl's brother's brand-new Jeep. My mother was furious. He just got his license last month. He was driving when he was 15 years old.

Dennis would have money like a grown man—hundreds of dollars. He used to not even care about money. Ten dollars used to be a lot of money to this boy. He hasn't seen my grandmother in two months and she lives right next door. My momma cries all the time now.

The worse thing is that he acts like those no-good little dope boys is his family. That girl and her family are all involved in selling drugs. Dennis screamed at me and told me that I don't know what I'm talking about. Well, people don't drive Mercedes Benz's, Saabs, Lincolns, and brand-new BMWs unless they're rich. That girl's mother drives a brand-new Mercedes and she works at some factory job—get real! Dennis spends the night over her house all the time. Her mother don't care. My mother called and told her mother to send Dennis home and that she didn't appreciate her letting Dennis live over there. The woman cursed momma out. . . .

Now Dennis's grades are dropping and he told me school ain't nothing. He's not the same boy. He doesn't hang with his old friends and he doesn't even play basketball anymore. My little brothers say he treats them real mean—he's not the same person. That crew mess is tearing our family apart.

My Uncle William works at the post office. He tried talking to Dennis. They talked about my father who died when we were really young. He told Dennis that my father would be really disappointed. Dennis got really mad and said he's moving in with that tramp. I wish the police, the mayor, or even the president would do something. . . . It's messed up!

SUBJECT: PARENTAL APPROVAL

Gail, 39, a mother of five (three boys, 20, 17, 16, and two girls, 21 and 15), addressed the issue of two of her sons' involvement with scavenger gangs. Asked by the interviewer if she approves of her sons belonging to a youth gang that might be involved with drug trade, she curtly announced:

I don't watch my boys all the time. But I trust them. . . . They're grown up and they're making it. Drugs? Gangs? Look here, you got a job for them? It's hard out here! My boys giving me nice things, why should I question them? Police, school, everybody always picking at them—they used to belong to a little silly group of boys calling themselves the Joes. But that ain't no big deal. Who said they're dealing drugs? Better selling than using. The way I see this whole mess is that people like my social worker, the bitch, don't want other folks to get anything nice in life.

My kids don't like school and they can't get no real good jobs so they got to make it in the street. The streets are tough, so you make however you can. Anyway, white folks and stuck-up niggahs keep all the good-paying jobs, houses and cars for themselves. I bet you got a good job? You asking questions for minimum wage? My nosey-ass social worker's always asking where's your boys? What they doing? They been in jail? Are your daughters pregnant? You got a man?

That ugly bitch don't care about nothing but cutting me off aid. I've already lost two dependents, 'cause one of my boys living with his girlfriend. So I told him you got to make up for the money I'm losing with you gone. Ms. Thang always trying to catch me doing something. Sure, my boys hang around with street boys. What you expect they do, go with some college boys? Now I tell my girls, get you a man with some money—that's the only thing that counts. My youngest, she's real smart. Her little boyfriend got a brand-new Pontiac 600STE and his own apartment and he's only 19. He's helping my boys get themselves established in business things. What's wrong with having nice things? I would love to have a nice house and car like other people.

I tell my girls, don't be no fool and get no babies like I did at 15. My oldest girl, she's 21 and she works at the gas company. She wants to marry this boy from work. But I think my young baby girls is smarter 'cause her little cute boyfriend got lots of money and he ain't stingy. . . . That boy gives us some nice gifts, yes sir. My boys tell me if they get hooked up, they going to buy me a big house and lots of new clothes and a brand new Cadillac. Why shouldn't I have nice things? I get tired of *seeing everybody else looking nice. It would be just great to go into a market and not shop with food stamps. People look at you like you ain't nothing. The cashiers act like you is poorer than anybody in the world. I went to the store and bought $200 worth of groceries with money from my babies and their new friends. Do I care where the money come from? No, I don't give one damn bit. It's money and it's my turn to get a piece of that money.*

I played numbers for the past twenty-four years, I played lotteries, charities, anything that might get me out of this dirty old building. Drugs—just business, a way to make it.

SUBJECT: THE VALUE OF AN EDUCATION

Kim, 16, works occasionally for her boyfriend and his corporate gang. She reflected on the value of education for herself and others:

School is cool, it's OK with me. My mother wants me to go to college 'cause I get good grades. The people I hang out with they got money and they didn't go to college. So I don't know if I want to go. . . . Charlotte, the girl across the street, went to college and graduated. She still living at home. She just got a job with Monkey Wards [Montgomery Ward] somewhere not in Detroit. She hates it. Her and my sister used to be tight. But ever since we started hanging with the fellas, her daddy act like we skeezers, you know? I got a cool counselor and she say I should go to college away from Detroit. But I like Detroit and I don't want to leave my friends or my boyfriend.

My boyfriend going to set me up in my own business when I graduate. My sister going to cosmetology school and we want to open up a hair salon and clothing shop. Now that would be slick. Lot of people are jealous 'cause I'm rolling. . . . I do favors and little business for my man. I've saved all my money when I work. So I really can't see college, 'cause I'm already straight. Me and my sister got real sweet clothes and my boyfriend is rolling hard. I've already ordered my new convertible Mustang, I can't wait to graduate. I look at Charlotte, she's driving an old 82 Delta that's all rusted. She ain't got no clothes worth talking about. Her boyfriend is some college prep boy that drives a little ugly-ass Toyota. My boys say it's a ho-car [laughing]. Then I look at my friends—they dressing clever, we riding in Beemers, Benzos and slick Jeeps. My momma is pretty proud of me. I'm straight, so I really can't see the need for any more education.

Even though Charlotte don't hang with us, you can tell she wants to get with us real bad. We look real good and we know it. I might go to college, but I rather set up my beauty business, and maybe then I'll go.

For me and my crew it's big fun at high school 'cause you get to show your clothes, jewelry, gold, things like that. My friends are making money right now. So they really don't even think about later or after school. You go to college to get a good job—right? Well, I got a good job. . . .

SUBJECT: VIOLENCE INVOLVED WITH GANGS

The interviewer asked Lamont, 13; Lawrence, 14; Kermit, 15; and Calvin, 16, if the scavenger gang life is violent.

Lamont remarked:

Violence? Man, if you got a crew you got to keep niggahs scared or they think you soft or like a little ho.

Hermit and Calvin concurred:

Beasting on niggahs is part of business. I heard how the [C-1] used to beat niggahs down with baseball bats. They would beat down on their own boys if they was dipping into the dope or doughski. I remember when everybody was talking about Andy Bopp and how he was popping junkies for his crew. The life is full of fucking mugs up. Gangsters got to pop suckers, you see that in the gangster movies.

Lawrence muttered:

You might have to tighten up your own brother or boy, if they start illing. The dudes in this crew some of them need to get popped, 'cause they play around too much. That's why we ain't making no paper. If we would get serious we could get paid like the big fellas. The Does take care of hos, perpetrators, real quick. But they don't fuck with nobody for silly-ass reasons.

Lamont agreed with Lawrence:

Yo, young Lawrence is straight if we did shit def like the big fellas then people would respect us. We should start popping dudes if they look at us wrong, then everybody would give us big play and say them Loes is bad.

SUBJECT: PARENTAL REACTION WHEN CHILDREN ARE INVOLVED WITH YOUTH GANGS

Tommy, 18, and his brother Delbert, 14, belong to a corporate gang. Their grandfather Sherman, 78, discovered their gang involvement. He told both of them that their gang membership was canceled if they wanted to continue living under his roof. Tommy left angrily, while Delbert decided to stay and sever his gang connections. Tommy's only comment was:

I got paper and I don't need to hear all that old-time bullshit about his house and ways.

Delbert indicated that the gang is not his only priority:

I rather stay home with granddaddy. He fusses and cusses but he's cool. Anyway, the crew get crazy and I ain't making big dough like Tommy. Really, they just treat me like a ho. I ain't standing on no corners in the winter or rain. Plus, if you think you snitching or saying something to the hook they'll beast on your ass. I don't really know shit and I'm glad.

Sherman, the boy's grandfather, responded to the question of parental responsibility:

The world done went crazy today. I don't know what these kids are doing today. My grandsons used to be good boys. But the neighborhood has changed. Tommy is driving fancy cars and carrying money like a rich man. He talking big these days. I asked him about the money and the fancy cars. He said his friends helped him get a good job. Now he was working after school as a clerk at this hardware store. He was talking about joining the Marines. Suddenly, he started dressing real fancy and running around with real strange characters. They would come by here driving some of them fancy Nazi cars. I told him, it only take a few seconds to get in trouble. He ain't listening to his old grandfather. No, sir. Now the younger boy, he started hanging around these bummy people. Fancy clothes don't hide no bums from me.

Tommy drove some little Japanese car home saying he paid for it with his money. That did it! I said, "How in the hell can you buy a damn thing?" I worked almost forty years at Ford and he's buying little plastic Jap cars. He tells me his boys bought cars and houses for their parents. Well, they all can go to hell. That's what's wrong with parents today—they're for sale. Either they robbing banks or selling dope to hop-heads. I ain't standing for no shit from my kids or grandkids. No, sir, I fought in the big war and I'm too god damn old to start letting kids tell me what they're going to do.

My daughter passed away four years ago, the boys' father was killed in Viet Nam. Before Tommy got with this bad bunch he was a good boy. But now he's acting like some ignorant-ass street bum. But I've warned him if the police get his friends and him, don't be crying, 'cause you did it, sonny boy.

Now, Tommy's best friend Preston, he's in with this no-good bunch, too. But Preston's momma ain't worth two dead flies, so I'm not surprised. People today don't give a damn about their kids. Preston's mother got a fancy car, big fur coats, and acting like nothing is wrong. I'll be damn if Tommy will get my approval—he's wrong and heading for trouble with that bunch of crooks. I've told him when he finishes running around with those no-good bums he can come home, but not until. Now, I got to make sure this other one, Delbert, gets back on the right track.

It's hard today raising kids in this world. Harder in Detroit with all this shooting and killing. Kids carrying guns—I might just move back to Alabama. Grown people helping kids do wrong, that's why you can't stop 'em today. Somebody needs to make these parents responsible, and somebody needs to get these young bums off the street cause problems, and that includes my Tommy if he's out there acting fool. He wasn't raised like that—no, sir, he was raised the right way!

SUBJECT: INNOCENT NON-GANG MEMBERS AND GANG LIFE

Mona, a mother of six, talked about her ordeal with youth gangs. Her oldest son Jeff, 16, belonged to the Roes. His gang has been accused of robbing several dope houses that belonged to an independent small drug dealer. The drug dealer has hired a notorious gang of young toughs to avenge the robberies. The hired gang has a reputation for being ruthless and deadly. Mona said:

It's been hell . . . the neighborhood is constantly having problems. Ain't easy raising kids during these times. I don't even like talking about it. I just want to be left alone with my kids. I don't need no trouble, especially from these crazy maniacs in these gangs. The kids can't even go to the rec center without some hoodlums bothering them. My youngest boy, Eugene, had his gym shoes taken off his feet one morning going to school. I'm worried all the time about my children. Jeffrey started hanging around the boys across the street. Those boys lived with their uncle, they always did whatever they wanted. Jeffrey started smoking, skipping school, and just acting real different.

Then last year some hoodlums firebombed those boys' house. Their uncle moved out after somebody came and shot the house up. Jeffrey was lucky that he wasn't over there. But he was mad and said he knew who did it. I told him to stay away from those boys. After those boys' uncle moved, they had Jeffrey and everybody including girls staying over there. I tried to get Jeffrey to leave them alone. They start running in and out of that house all times of day and night. A neighbor, Mr. Smith, said they were selling dope. My daughter said they were selling dope and that Jeffrey was helping. Right after that, the house was firebombed again. My oldest daughter was threatened at school by some niggahs calling themselves the Terminators. They're looking for Jeffrey and those other boys. Now I find out that Jeffrey belongs to some gang called the Roes. I didn't even know until you younger kids told me.

69

I want to move, but where? The worst thing was those crazies shot into my neighbor's house next door, got the wrong house. Thank God, nobody got hurt. I found Jeffrey hiding over his little fast girlfriend's. I told him that his mess had caused me grief and put everybody in our house in danger. He started crying, talking about how sorry he was. Well, tell Mrs. Jackson next door about sorry after getting her house shot up. Tell his sisters and brothers about sorry after having them fools drive by our house threatening everyone. I told Jeffrey not to come home unless he was out of that damn gang.

Jeffrey told his brothers and sisters that he was going to buy a new car and house and other things. But I told him I don't want anything from that blood money. He can live with those dope rats and never come home, far as I'm concerned. If I could, I would move back down south. These crazy dope people don't care about who they hurt. I don't know what happened. But I'll tell you one thing—no dope people, including if they are my own children, are coming into this house.

SUBJECT: DOING BUSINESS WITH YOUTH GANGS

The interviewer discussed with a scavenger gang the effects of gangs on neighborhood business. Corkey explains his crew's feelings regarding business in their neighborhood.

The a-rabbs own all the stores in our hood. They hire the cuties to work the lotto tickets and won't give no dudes nothing but flunkey jobs. The a-rabbs sell shit way too high . . . and they be dissing bloods, talking real fucked-up to us bloods. Our crew has to check some of them a-rabbs who think they got big juice 'cause they got guns. Some of them are real down with some rollers. They talk bad to us and then give the police free pops and other shit and tell lies on us after they done dissed us.

Ain't no stores hiring nobody from my crew. One time a a-rabb pulled his gun on me and some of the fellas in his store. We left 'cause they weren't bullshitting. They will cap a blood over some potato chips. But later we'll fix them punk-ass a-rabbs. How come they come into our hood and start stores acting like all the bloods ain't shit. So if somebody robs or beats on people, maybe they shouldn't go to the a-rabbs' stores [laughing].

Gary concluded:

The only business in our hood that bloods run is caine for

*the dope fiends. Selling 'caine makes more doughski than little
bullshit shops in the hood. The crews like the Roes are making real
hard doughski, and they are the real live businesses in our hood
and city.*

SUBJECT: RUTHLESS, VIOLENT BEHAVIOR OF YOUTH GANGS

Terrell Evans, 29, was serving a prison term for murder.
Evans had a confrontation with a gang of juveniles in his
neighborhood. Evans and his best friend, Lester Rollins, were
operating a small after-hour operation (a blind pig). Rollins
summarized the ordeal that ended in the death of a 15-year-
old gang leader:

> *These young boys were like crazed animals. . . . The boy that
was the leader, he wasn't really 15, he wasn't like no teenager,
he was a cold-blooded man, a ruthless killer.*

> *We was running a little private party—selling drinks, play-
ing cards, shooting dice—you know, just a little good times.
Anyway, one of them gang boys started robbing our customers.
Those boys were terrorizing the whole neighborhood. They did
whatever they pleased. So me and Terrell tried to talk with them,
you know, talk street, man to man, to these young punks. We
tried to be fair and work these little problems out.*

> *The gang came by our place when we were out one day. They
stole our video and stereo equipment. Terrell was pissed and
put out the word that he wanted our shit brought back or he
was going to tighten their young asses up. The bold-ass little
bastards sent word back that they did it, and fuck us! The
leader, Howard, came by one afternoon and told us he didn't
have the video and stereo. Terrell got so mad he pulled his gun
out. Howard said that he might as well shoot him 'cause if he got
out his crew would come back and take our asses out. Terrell got
scared and shot Howard six times. You could tell how nervous
and scared Terrell was and that Howard wasn't bullshitting. It just
happened—like that.*

> *After the police arrested Terrell, the shit really got crazy.
Howard's crew came by the house looking for Terrell. Nobody
was home. They shot up the house and set it on fire. Nobody
saw nothing in the neighborhood. Old people, young people,*

everybody is scared of these gang boys. Times ain't like when I was young. These young boys are cold—you can see it in their eyes. Terrell is safer in prison. Anyway, what could he do? If that little fool had got back to his crew we would have been dead for sure. People can't call the police on all these crazy gang boys.

SUBJECT: LEAVING A GANG

Mitchell, 20, described the plight and frustrations of leaving an urban youth gang.

Man, belonging to a crew is the only way for many mugs. My crew been trying to hit the action like those big doughski fellas. If you get it on with big dough, life is straight. But I'm tired and things getting too ill for making it. I tried boxing when I was 14. I was pretty good, but the coach at the gym was trying to make us go back to school. I wanted to box, later for school! What school got to do with boxing?

I've been living with two skeezers, but they illing all the time. You know what every skeezer want? A fella who's rolling hard, clocking doughski. The only fellas doing that is the ones rolling with the big fellas. They got connections, big fella connections, lawyers, clothes, def-ass rides and the skeezers love 'em. You got to have the paper or you ain't shit in this world. My crew just can't hit the big time. We stick up anybody on the streets, break in houses, sell hot shit like TVs, videos, gold jewelry, car tires, microwaves, whatever. But the hook knew our shit like they belonged to our crew. They was on our asses all the time. That's another reason we can't get over. Our crew can't get no respect 'cause the niggahs in our crew are dumb, they illing doing shit that's real ill, making it easy for the hook to catch us. I'm on probation for selling twenty dollars worth of crack—ain't that a bitch?

I got this aunt who's illing about me get into this training pro-gram and making something of myself. She say vote, vote, vote for the Democratic ticket. So me and two of my boys go and get into this training school for chauffeurs. My jive-ass court-appointed lawyer said the judge would like me and the fellas if we got into one of these programs. My aunt is talking about Jesse Jackson being president. I don't know nothing about voting or Jesse Jackson. President? Man, ain't no whitey letting no niggah be president. No way! But I'm trying to survive so I get in the bullshit, phoney-talking program. It's fraudulent as a mug. They want big doughski, they talk about paying for everything—bullshit! Mutha-fuckas give you a loan to pay the tuition. Me and my boy Roscoe told the man we wanted def jobs after we graduated. I figured this training program might be a way out of here. My aunt was talking shit about voting and being part of people working for a living. She was dissing me, so I told her that the punks at the school were one hundred percent fake, fake like the mug. She started dissing my life and I told her that all them big fellas be dissing the poor little niggahs on the stroll.

Ain't no difference 'tween us and any other crew. Look at the president and his crew. I bet the president got some cuties and being slinging him some candy 'caine. My aunt talks about civil rights and Reverend King. She said he was real, you know, he was down. But ain't nobody real no more, everybody be dissing everybody. After I caught my case, I figured the school might help. But they fraudulent, you know Roscoe can't read anything and they gave him his GED diploma 'cause they guaranteed a GED and driving certification. They don't care about nothing but getting paid—that's all. We graduated from the school and lying fraudulent school people started shitty yappin' about working at some stiff-ass chauffeur company for $4.35 a hour. When we first got to school, they was talking about ten dollar a hour plus big tips. We go the company and they don't want us for regular drivers but substitute drivers. Check this, the punk-ass mutha-fuckas dissed us and told us to wash the limos. Wash cars—that's what I went to school for? Fuck it! Just another trick! I told my aunt, yeah, remember that training program, well, they want bloods to wash cars for $4.35. Me and Roscoe tried to join the Army cause our crew made a real def mistake—they got caught robbing a private party of one of the [C-2] boys. Now our crew is out cold. Everybody and anybody want a piece of our asses. So we tried to join the army. They was out cold, said we couldn't pass the written test so they didn't want us. The sergeant down at the recruiting station said the army wasn't taking nobody that couldn't read or write no more. I can read OK. I didn't finish school, but I can count my paper.

But fuck the army, too. I don't know what I'm going to do now. I thought a lot about trying to hook up with some big crew. I know some skeezers that got some tight connections with some big fellas. I'm trying to get next to one of them. Maybe this time I'll get a break. I ain't getting tricked no more by no lying fake artist like that training program. I just want some real paper, not some $4.35 an hour bullshit job!

COMMUNITY RESPONSE

The community at large has responded to the urban youth gangs in a variety of ways. The overall reaction has been one of dismay and confusion. Many neighborhoods have experienced a steady decline since the riot of 1967. Social institutions grapple with increasing pressure from the depressed socioeconomics of this industrialized urban environment. The church, school, family, criminal justice system, and business sector have all been adversely affected by urban youth gangs.

The devastation of the auto industry has placed a tremendous burden on the community. Everyday problems of any urban center are strenuous, but the massive loss of jobs, middle-class flight, and increasing crime, have left many Detroit neighborhoods barren and hopeless. The nucleus of any community is also the heart of America—the family.

Earlier interviews have recounted the hopelessness that many families feel and face in Detroit. The erosion of the family and its values has had a domino effect on other social institutions. This study reveals that the overall deterioration of the community is exacerbated by youngsters involved in major crime.

The concept of the Community Team Effort aligns the major components of the community into an infrastructure that can work to reduce or reverse the drastic changes that are fueling urban youth gangs. The key to the Community Team Effort must begin with an understanding of the community and its many components and needs. Although the *parens patriae* doctrine* is an old concept, it is suitable for addressing this problem at the onset of 1990 because too many parents are abdicating their responsibilities.

The family has changed in the past thirty years. Detroit has felt the burden of not only younger families but poorer families. Some neighborhoods have attempted to keep their close-knit networks despite the way urban gangs have changed them in recent years.

A retired postal worker spoke discouragingly about the once-structured neighborhood and his street's block club.

> *I've lived on this street for the past thirty-four years. I just don't know what happened. The people have changed, the city, the kids . . . everything has changed. My kids are grown and I've got grand-kids. I never dreamed that I would have problems on this street. I was block club president and watched each other's houses, children, dogs. . . .*
>
> *It's only a few of us left on this block, the new people aren't friendly like when I first moved here. Gangs? We never had no gang mess in this neighborhood. No, sir! Sure, we've seen hoodlums but everybody had a few hoodlums . . . young hoods respected our street and block club. We didn't have none of this shooting up houses, innocent folks getting shot. . . . Drugs made this town crazy. These dope peddlers bought up these kids and now we can't even sit on our porch. . . . The people on this block used to watch how kids talked and played like they were their own. Now if you say something to one of these kids they'll cuss you out. I know some of these parents got to know what's going on. Little kids running the streets all times of the day and night. Where's their mommas? I'd say the drugs, the dope is what made everybody crazy. You see young boys wearing gold chains, looking like grown men. Use to see kids playing*

---

parens patriae (Latin)—the sovereign power of guardianship over minors and insane or incompetent people as vested in the state.

basketball, baseball or skipping rope . . . not anymore. They all look old, mean and serious.

The dope and the hoodlums done made everybody stay in their houses. You can't go anywhere cause of the dope trouble. It's more of the dope pushers than it is police. You can't go nowhere cause the dope addicts breaking into your house, and the dope gangs will kill you on the streets.

An elementary school teacher, a twenty-one-year veteran, addressed the impact of street gangs at the elementary level:

You hear about crews, I guess that's a gang . . . these students know about crews, dope, guns, cars like grownups. Little girls dress like older girls in high school. I think the impact has been on the whole educational system. I've seen kids young as seven, eight wearing expensive Nike, Reeboks, you name it and these students know about it and they got it. We don't get interested parents or students anymore. I think all these students think about is money, money and big cars, and they're not even old enough to drive. It's simply the role model for many of these kids are the successful drug people. Boys and girls are preoccupied with the glamour of this life style. This neighborhood used to have stores, jobs for kids. We've lost so many small businesses and they haven't been replaced. The empty stores, the abandoned houses, are depressing. Fear controls the kids and the teachers. These are elementary children and they know about death. Many of these students have known someone that has been victimized by violence. They see drugs, violence, everyday in real life. They see violence on television. These kids are under constant pressure that didn't exist thirty years ago.

I used to look forward to teaching every day . . . now my concern is my car alarm and leaving school in one piece. These kids can't learn in this atmosphere. I have friends who teach junior high and high school and it's worse. I've seen kids that have serious problems over the years. But today the bad ones are different. Some of the parents are so young that they should still be in high school. Parent-teacher conferences are poorly attended. If we don't have parent support you can't expect successful results.

A retired high school counselor said that the everyday student is a victim. "The kids who aren't part of the thugs and drugs are paying a horrible price. I'm just puzzled the public can expect anyone to teach or learn while you have major distractions in the schools."

Another counselor, who spoke only on the condition of anonymity, targeted parents and students as the root of school problems.

> *These bad attitudes, nasty ways, are supported by parents many times. When I first started in this business you took threats with a grain of salt. Today I take everything said as a possibility. Recently I was told by a 16-year-old girl that I better watch how I talked to her or her crew might visit me. Now years ago I would have contacted her parents. Forget it. Sure there are many caring, concerned parents. But the ones that should come to school never come. The ones that come and attack you as the educator are really the frightening ones. They blame everyone for the student's problems. I had a mother tell me that kids will be kids, after her sons had threatened a teacher, security personnel, students, and myself. The families have changed, the attitudes have changed. Today the teachers are wrong, the counselor is wrong, the principal is wrong, the police are wrong, the judge is wrong, the world is wrong. It doesn't surprise me, unfortunately the attitudes of many parents is the key to their kids' bad relations with the world. Some parents consider all of this concern over child's play. Making excuses, spoiled brats, violent behavior, creates the atmosphere for poor teaching, counseling, and worst, poor students. It's such a shame . . . the bad ones making money showing how crime pays, undoing everything we're trying to do. All I can say is that it's not getting any better.*

An attorney in private practice who is married to a Detroit dentist, works with several community groups and is very active in her church. She has observed that street lure is powerful.

> *I work with our youth choir and you have young boys who come from good homes identifying with the street crowd. The young church girls are caught up in the street life unlike when I was in school at that age. These are good youngsters from solid Christian homes . . . so if they can be tempted what does that say about the kids from unstable homes? Some of our church boys leave the church and become entangled in the fast world*

78

of drugs. What's really scary is when they come back to the church and show off their new-found wealth.

As an attorney I know the system can't handle the situation as it stands presently. And honestly, it's mainly young black men that I'm seeing . . . they are so young it's depressing. I have a brother who teaches high school and he talks about how the bad ones are quiet in school. These dope pushers use children, turn them into monsters, and we're just dumbfounded. I feel hopeless and helpless. It's like the bad guys are winning and it's eating up our city. You go to the malls, you see 'em; go to the video stores, the gang people are taking over. And the worst part is that kids are accepting these people as successful people! My friends have problems with their children and they're in solid neighborhoods and schools. You wouldn't believe the money or cars that some of these drug boys have. My best friend whose daughter is in a Catholic girls' school, had to call the police to stop some rough-looking boys in Mecedes Benz's from harassing their family. The boys were trying to court her daughter. They met her at somebody's house in the suburbs. Now the girls' school is being flooded by BMWs, Mercedes, Jeeps, Corvettes and drug boys. This is unbelievable . . . and some of the school girls are actually dating these dope peddlers. I can't fathom a young girl from a good home socializing with the likes of these hoodlums. The impact on this city has been crushing . . . crack cocaine, the killing, and the young lives that are being ruined.

A supervisor in the auto industry, who owned a small party store in the northwest section of Detroit, related his experience with today's gangs:

I was a tough kid, belonged to a street gang, did time in training school when I was sixteen. When I got out I joined the army, did my bit and came back to the plant. My wife worked at Hudson's downtown and we were saving money for a party store. I took a second job as a janitor for about six years until we had our second kid. GI bill helped me buy the store. Got it from a Jewish guy who was scared after the riots in '67. When I took over we had five big apartment buildings within two blocks. There were also about a dozen four-family buildings and several small apartments. We had plenty of customers. The school complex is only two blocks away and the school kids always buying potato chips, pop, candy. We were so happy. This was our dream come true.

Then about the fall of 1968 things started to change slowly. That damn heroin started. By 1969 some of the more established homes started moving. The apartment people were changing from working to shaky types. The plant layoffs caused lots of people to leave town. By 1970 junkies were breaking into everybody's place. The store was broken into for the first time in June 1970. We had never had trouble. I always got along with the so-called bad boys. Hell, I was once one of them. They came into the store and buy pop, candy, cigarettes, like anybody else. If they were short of money I'd let them slide . . . they never gave me any trouble; they weren't gangs like today. They were just dropouts, street fellas with nothing to do. When heroin took the streets the neighborhood really got hurt . . . real bad scene.

I had to get burglar alarms, bars, steel doors—it was like war. The people started changing in the neighborhood, the school kids changed—it just seemed like another time and place. Junkies started coming into the store. They would steal like crazy and they scared my wife. Finally, we got robbed by some idiots with shotguns. That did it. I knew then I had to sell the place. By 1974 the neighborhood was empty, the apartments were abandoned like many of the homes. It was scary. The people of the older established families moved or locked themselves in the house.

I couldn't sell, so I had bulletproof glass installed. We had to have guns behind the counter. All we wanted was to break even and get out. The street is quiet but it's dead quiet, not peaceful quiet. We got through the seventies and heroin. But things got bad, actually worse, in 1980. That's when these young boys started selling dope. Young boys like 14 running up and down the apartment building on the corner. That building is full of dope addicts. They started taking over houses and junkies were selling hot televisions, lawn mowers car stereos and tape decks. I don't know if it was gangs or what, but I can tell you this much. It was young boys, little boys running out of cabs, cars selling something over at the corner. My wife stopped coming to the store cause she was so scared of these young idiots. They come into the store and act real sneaky, didn't talk just buy things and leave. But you could feel something real strange about these kids. Now the bad ones would be acting up, but these dope fellas just stare at you as if you weren't real . . . it was real strange.

I talked to some old buddies of mine and they understood exactly how I felt these new fellas operated. By 1982 the dope had taken over the street. I couldn't sell because the neighborhood looked like a ghost town. Dope houses were the new neighbors. A woman who had lived on the street since 1952 tried organizing a block club to fight the dope boys. She got no support, everybody was scared, so she moved. What can I do? In the past few years the only customers I have are the school children and the dope crowd. The kids are in the middle of all this mess. What can a parent do? I thought 1969 was bad, but now you see young fellas driving brand new cars up to the school. I used to sit out in front of the store and watch the kids, talk to the neighbors, mailman, but nobody is around and if I sit in front of the store one of these idiots will mow me down with a machine gun and won't give a damn if he killed me or some innocent kids. Impact? The impact has been like a giant monster destroying everything in its way. . . . These young boys didn't start this mess but they sure as hell are part of it. . . .

A high school senior reflected on being a student with urban gangs:

They're everywhere, big time crews, jit crews, guys who pretend they're rolling, girls who love crews . . . it's bad. Teachers know, security knows, janitors know, principals and counselors know, but what can they do? The guys who are rolling hard, they have bodyguards, big Benz's, sharp clothes, guns, friends, pretty girls . . . they've got it all. I've got girlfriends who go with crew boys, and they have money all the time. I have my friends and we don't like the rolling crowd. It's hard to even party without the crew crowd coming and spoiling everything. I'm not impressed with their cars, money, or clothes. But I've seen lots of people staring at their clothes and cars. My parents would die if I came home with a roller. Anyway, dope boys think they own you if they buy you anything. I think school would be a lot more pleasant if they weren't allowed to wear their jewelry and drive their mopeds and fancy cars. It's harder to learn or pay attention to school when you have the class checking out the big rollers. I wish they would just leave the city and stop all their shooting and killing. Some of the guys are really good students and friendly. But some dope gangs are crazy and I just stay out of their way.

The scariest thing is that you never know when they're going to get into an argument and start shooting. If they come to a party I leave right away. My boyfriend goes to college, and I'll just be glad when I leave the city from this shooting, fighting between crews. Last year I was at a football game and some crew boys got mad and the next thing I knew they're shooting in the stands and girls are crying and screaming. After that my parents said no more football or basketball games. It's so unfair, can't do this, I hate it, because of some crews I'm punished and I haven't done anything. Me and my friends just wait until college for some regular fun.

A community activist and social worker said:

The lost jobs have caused families to crumble. People have given up hope—many of these kids are victims of homes that have never had a regular family life style. Many of the kids see drug abuse by their family members. When parents are preoccupied with drugs they aren't the best parents. The things we take for granted like rules for staying off the neighbors' lawn—these kids haven't been taught these rules. The glamour of the drug life is very appealing. It's different for these young boys when they see day in and day out fancy cars driven by their peers. The temptation is great for adults in the drug business, so we can't be shocked when youngsters get lured into the drug business.

This community needs jobs and good housing to recreate strong neighborhoods. When homes are strong, people working, it helps as a role model for young men. Sure, these boys are getting violent and selling drugs. Do you expect a kid to work for minimum wage? It's especially difficult to combat drug money for these youngsters. The problem of these youngsters is that nobody is really sure of what to do. Leaving the city isn't going to solve a damn thing. I personally think if we had jobs it would make quite a difference. When these youngsters have nothing to do and nowhere to work, the only answer is to sell drugs. When this community was employed it was more stable. When youngsters see older men not working, it's the wrong image, the signal that says it's hopeless.

A fourteen-year veteran of the local law enforcement community more trouble:

Gangs, groups, clubs, crews, call it what you want, we got trouble. The impact on the community is very sad and serious. The young ones know they can do whatever is possible. Dope, murder, fight, it's all the same. They go in one door and presto, they are out! The system doesn't work anymore. It's frustrating as hell. I see young arrogant punks bragging about their connections, their lawyers. They don't respect us or anybody. Why should they? You see it every day in court—the judges let them go. The know it, other kids know it, their parents know it, the whole city knows we can't do anything in reality.

A lot of guys are so angry 'cause we're damned by everybody. And all these arrogant punks carry guns. Remember the automatic sentence of two years for carrying a firearm? Ha! It's like everybody has a gun, even the real little ones. We should have closed those little crews down when they first started this dope crap. Now everybody is worried. I tell you, life in the streets is different. It doesn't matter a teenager or adult, they all know that Michigan courts and jails are overworked and overcrowded. How can we do our jobs of enforcement when they're laughing 'cause the law is overcrowded? I don't see nothing promising or changing. Everything is getting worse.

The assistant to the pastor at a Baptist Church, Rev. Floyd D. Smith, addressing the lure of materialism on youngsters in the church, said:

There is a shift in the focus of some good kids. I can remember when many students separated themselves from the rough crowd. They made a special effort to dress differently and behave in a manner that was reflective of good citizenry. I can see how some children are blending from the presence of the new popular street culture. The expensive gym shoes, the expensive cars, the large amounts of money and the seeming popularity of their peer grouping. We all should be concerned when good children are taking notice of those in the fast lane. It's not easy being a youngster in Detroit . . . the poverty, the drop-out rate, and the high unemployment doesn't discriminate against the young.

I sense that unlike earlier times in this city many people, including the children, feel hopeless. The gang business fills the vacuum left by unemployment and poverty. Gangs have existed before Detroit's current problems. Many young people seeking their identities, family needs, friendships, and rewards have substituted gangs. The church has not been the beacon for gang participants in general. I have pondered the reasons that those who might need our direction, guidance, aren't being

83

assisted. I feel that we're missing the target in a sense. In some ways the lure is for the good kids to be attracted by the evil trappings of the drug dealers. The use of children as employees of this wretched industry is repulsive. The whole community is impacted by the business of gangsterism and dope. Far too many role models are talking one type of idealistic rhetoric and living another. Our young people are aware of the superficial, deceiving rhetoric. We must lead by realistic examples!

A Detroit attorney and former member of the State of Michigan Corrections Commission, Brunetta Brandy, said:

The impact of the drug culture and violence on young black males is very depressing. When you realize the young ages of these young boys and men one can only sense that society is in a very serious dilemma . . . mind you not Detroit or Michigan, but American society.

A retired social worker and former director of Neighborhood Service City of Detroit, Georgia Brown, stated:

There has been a collapse of neighborhoods as we once knew them. A sense of hopelessness pervades the inner city. Young men are behaving in ways that are opposed to the traditional upbringings in the black community. A lack of employment, education, and of the traditional family have caused our youth extensive damage.

I'm not certain why young people are behaving in such violent and hostile ways suddenly. The family plays such an important role and we need moral leadership on all fronts. Moral leadership sets the tempo for our youth. When children see adults abusing drugs, people, food, and children it sends the wrong signals to our youngsters. Our leaders must stand tall and be moral. From political leaders, from the president of the United States on down, we must have leadership by example. Mothers and fathers in the past provided strong examples of positive role models . . . today leadership has been replaced with material objects. How much did it cost? What's your title? And what type of car? These things are more important than our children today. Some youngsters know how to con everybody in the criminal justice system. Too many people in this situation become jaded and frustrated. You see kids getting worse everyday and you know the gang boys impress them more than you ever will. . . .

It's getting harder and harder convincing myself that I'm making any progress.

A probation officer observed:

It's getting harder to steer young people in the right direction. The crews make it hard. Drugs play a role that Chrysler used to fill. A kid in the street looks at the big money, big car, without the task of going into higher education or skill job training. We're losing the battle with these kids. The jails are overcrowded and the youth home is packed. What can we do? A kid learns real quick that the system can't hold kids.

As long as Mercedes Benz's, custom Corvettes, designer clothes, are the rewards and there is virtually no punishment . . . the kids will continue to pursue their idea of success. Let's face it, there's not a lot of opportunities for these kids in this city. Earning $3.50 an hour compared to hundreds, or better yet, thousands of dollars, talks in any language. It's simple. It's a job—real work to these kids. Right or wrong, it's a job.

In the Emmy Award winning television documentary, "Kids and Heroin," members of the criminal justice system shared their views on youth gangs. Judge Gladys Barsimian said, "It's pretty hard talking to a youngster about frying hamburgers at McDonald's when he has $10,000 in cash on him." Detroit Police Commander Gilbert Hill emphasized that one corporate gang's attitude toward the public showed a total disregard for human life . . . shooting into innocent bystanders in pursuing their targets.

Detroit Police Commander Warren Harris, discounting the romantic image of the same corporate gang, observed, "They're no Robin Hoods—Robin Hood took from the rich and gave to the poor. They take from the poor . . . many times hurting the poor." Another former Detroit policeman, Robert De Faw, who headed the Drug Enforcement Agency in Detroit, indicated that this same corporate organization demanded strict discipline of not using drugs. "They enforced that rule through physical beatings, sometimes fatal."

Local attorney Otis Culpepper, in his interview during "Kids and Heroin," revealed how pervasively the image of drug traffickers has attracted inner city youth. Culpepper tells of how he was approached by a youngster volunteering his services for "rolling." The young man had assumed that since Culpepper was driving a very expensive foreign automobile that he was a drug pusher. Despite debates regarding the depth of Detroit's drug problem, Culpepper's solicitation by the youngster shows how many of these youths' perception of success and successful role models is distorted. Later during Culpepper's interview, he underscored how, despite efforts by joint law enforcement agencies, the drug gang problem continued. Federal indictments supposedly dismantled Detroit's premier corporate gang in 1982. Culpepper said, "Business was back on Dexter the next day after the indictments as usual." "Kids and Heroin" summarized the impact on Detroit when inner city youth merged into major criminals.

William Sparks, an advertising consultant said:

> Our community is not safe any more, a terrible influence has fallen on these kids. We have eroded in our values, a breakdown of authority. The community is so fragmented . . . it's a different community. A lot of transient people, families on the move, no religion, no structure, no respectability, no home training. Before going away to college, I had no problem walking home late at night in my old Detroit neighborhood. Sure we had bullies, gang boys, but they never bothered women or little kids. And we didn't have guns in those days. Neighbors were like aunts and uncles. Lots of discipline and respect during that period.
>
> Today I'm working with young people during some of our campaigns and there is a "new" attitude . . . mind you the music and young people only reflect society. We need to stop and reevaluate ourselves. . . .

A high school teacher, speaking on condition that her identity would be kept hidden, explained, "You can't really expect me or any teacher to function under the stress of drugs, gangs, and unruly students. . . . I'm just going through the motions, and I hate it."

John Eliott, president of the Detroit Teachers Federation, understands the concerns and fears of teachers. The school system has changed drastically in the past thirty years. Some educators are concerned that school violence has taken its toll on the public school, students, and personnel. Eliott concurred that the city and the system had changed over the years. He noted that without parental support, not much will happen. A high-school cafeteria worker responded:

> Crews or gangs, whatever you call 'em, it's bad in and out of school. These young boys are crazy and the girls are getting crazy like the boys. Everybody is fighting and they're all ready to fight over nothing. I'm only twenty-three but they treat me like I'm their age, no respect at all. Some kids running with crews 'cause it's cool, some 'cause they need protection. But for some it's like a family or a chance to become something for a change . . . it's their chance to be a star.

Erlaine Taylor, a retired school administrator and teacher noted:

> There has been a decline in terms of a positive relationship between parents and the school. When I first started teaching the profession was very respected in the community. Students were expected to respect teachers, adults, and the school. Parents were supportive of the teacher at that time. Today it seems that many parents don't care. In return teachers have changed—many young teachers are responding to the negatives.
>
> Television, the excitement, pimps, prostitutes, sports people, are the images the children are exposed to day in and day out. It's very frustrating to see the decline of so many young children. Education has such a limited appeal to many parents and students. It's as if they resent education; there's a subtle feeling that educators are elite. The lure of the streets is stronger than ever. When young children see expensive cars and clothes that cost more than those of their parents, teachers, principals, or anyone else in the community, they believe that this is correct. American leaders are not reflecting qualities of brotherly love. Success is money and power . . . these children are acting out the violence and cruelty that their parents and leaders have displayed. Their home life is shot, no love, violence, and cruelty. So it's no wonder that they come to school ready to hurt someone. It's very hard to teach under that type of pressure. The teaching profession has felt the pressure and burden of the changed student. Some teachers have developed the attitude of "It's a job. I got mine, you can get yours."

87

We must do something real soon . . . it's not only the kids engaged in criminal activities but the whole community suffers.

The tradition of groups of young rabble-rousers has evolved into serious problems represented by scavenger and corporate-type gangs. The territorial turf zones for juveniles has new meaning today. The inner city has become a war zone. The major changes in Detroit have been brought about by forces within the city and from outside. Urban gangs and their influences are part of that change from within. The erosion of the inner city was exacerbated by the 1967 riots and that civil disorder has continued into the present. Youngsters from displaced neighborhoods are now spread throughout the city. The inner city community is reverberating from an explosion of poverty, poor education, and violent crime. The intermixture of the inner city has given way and become a homogeneous core of the underclass. As the home has disintegrated, the erosion of hope and morals has increased.

The urban youngster has lost the social controls that existed as recently as the 1960s. Perhaps the feelings of many gang members and non-gang members is best addressed by a 16-year-old former gang member of a notorious corporate gang:

> Sure you see people with nice things and good jobs. But that's them, I'm not going to live for a long time. If a crew don't get you, something will. Out here life is happening fast and if you moved the wrong way or somebody thinks you moved wrong—it's over! Neighbors? Neighbors is for my grandmother. I ain't got the time. Church? People trying to get neat on Sunday and dissing people on Monday. School? Me, ain't got the time . . . anyway I know and they know—you know? Job? I had a job, making crazy paper. But you'll say it was against the law. So now I'm working for some bullshit youth corps that my fake-ass probation officer made me go to. This ain't no job and this ain't living. I'd be happier rolling, having cash, and having with my crew. So what if I get taken out? At least I had my own shit. . . . Would you work for some $3.35 a hour when you know you can make $300 a hour? Naw, you would be rolling 'cause that's the American way. Community? What's that? Only community I know is my boys—when we get together that's my church, home, and community!

The greater community embraces the welfare of all its citizens. The socioeconomics of Detroit created diverse communities. When inner-city residents observed prosperity all around them they desired to become part of that community. When opportunities were blocked, or perceived as blocked, those views festered and resulted in hollowed-out communities that have been eroding daily since 1967. Community must mean more than people and houses in a particular geographic area. Communities are the life lines of any city. Urban gangs, left unchecked, will continue to cause violence, crime, and depression. This study has touched upon the vital parts of the larger community. More research is needed. Unfortunately, the problems that existed in 1943 and 1967 still have healthy roots in 1989. The communities and their remaining neighborhoods must be rebuilt and revitalized in order to reestablish the much-needed social controls any real community must have.

FINAL ANALYSIS

This study has traced the complex evolution of Detroit's youth gangs. There is a great need to examine and analyze the reasons for this escalating problem in America. Urban America is in combat, fighting social and economic battles that have been going on for the past seventy years. Society needs to be cautious and honest before attempting to answer the questions arising from urban centers such as Detroit.

Detroit is unique because it has no strong gang legacies like Los Angeles and Chicago. Yet some neighborhoods have roots of third- and fourth-generation gangs. A former resident of the city spoke of how his neighborhood had changed. "The old neighborhood had working class, middle class, professionals, and lower class integrated—now the neighborhood is one-dimension, socially and economically."

It's not unusual that during an earlier period some neighborhoods had no gangs. In some neighborhoods the social constraints in the 1950s and 1960s eroded during the 1970s; by the 1980s many of these communities had very little control and had grown indifferent about living with crime. Scavenger gangs have always existed in some form.

91

DETROIT COMMUNITIES

In *Detroit: Race and Uneven Development,* Darden et al. underscored the uneven development and changing demography of Detroit that included white flight to the suburbs, differential use of public funds, and racism. But, because many immigrants found good jobs in the auto industry, this feeling of isolation was tolerable for many new Detroiters.

In the African-American communities, however, segregation and isolation were one. African-Americans, many of whom migrated from an overt southern segregation, found the northern version of separate but equal at first more comfortable to live with. Detroit had established one of the oldest African-American middle classes in America where many owned small businesses. Doctors, dentists, insurance people, ministers, and teachers were needed because of the large number of workers in the auto plants. Those who lived in the working and middle-class African-American neighborhoods understood and accepted the isolation of segregation while the unemployed, uneducated African-American created by the migrating flood from the south was overcrowding the limited low income housing.

A retired auto worker explained the old segregated neighborhoods:

> Folks used to room in houses and save money to buy their own places. I can remember in the 1950s when I bought my house from this Jewish fellow. I had saved for twelve years, rooming at a woman's house over on Erskine. You had to be sure and not live near those big apartment buildings where all them welfare folks lived. Those kids would be all over the place. They didn't know nothing about grass or shrubbery. So when I looked for my house I just made certain there wasn't any housing projects or big apartments full of kids. . . .

What he spoke of, housing projects and big apartment buildings full of kids, was at that time the foundation of the underclass in Detroit. Not everyone who lived in those conditions remained there, though many were predestined by the wars of invisible America to stay. The isolation of the housing projects in the inner city has had a rippling effect on the city up to this very day. Overcrowded and isolated, the lower-class dwellers had no choice but to live in the housing projects. Urban renewal and integration in the 1960s passed by this group of African-Americans. Although the community at large was isolated by segregation, the lower class was ignored and abandoned not only by race, but also by class.

Miraculously, the isolation of the African-American community didn't cause the majority to feel separated from America. That could easily have been possible because of the strong sense of community similar to that held by Italian-Americans and other ethnic groups. Despite segregation and Jim Crow laws, African-Americans had many role models in Detroit and beyond—Joe Louis, Jackie Robinson, Father Divine, Prophet Jones, Dorothy Dandridge, Lena Horne, Ella Fitzgerald, Carter G. Woodson, W. E. B. DuBois, John White, Rev. C. L. Franklin, and many others. Because of segregation African-Americans did not deviate from the isolation to which they were relegated.

During the 1980s, children and parents became increasingly frustrated and isolated from the mainstream of both America and African America. As Merton[1] had contended in his strain theory, children from the underclass were frustrated, especially when exposed to the riches of our society.

The media have played a very significant role in educating people in our society. With the technology of video recorders, video monitors, contemporary movies, and television, there is very little dichotomy between the haves and the have nots from the media perspective. Whereas middle-class America desires the better things in life and pursues them via jobs, college education, business loans, and savings, the underclass can realistically choose from very few avenues to pursue the American rags-to-riches story.

EDUCATION

The reality for many in the African-American community is that the underclass has given up all hopes and desires of achieving success by legitimate means. Historically, the youngsters who leave school early are more likely to join scavenger gangs. Scavengers in this study had very high drop-out rates compared to corporates.

Michigan has a school drop-out rate of 22 percent between the ninth and twelfth grades. This rate varies greatly, ranging from zero percent in some districts to well over 50 percent in the Detroit public schools.[2] A Michigan Department of Education study shows that school districts with high drop-out rates are more likely to be urbanized and have lower community wealth than are districts with low drop-out rates. In addition, dropping out is more frequent in minority populations.[3] From 1976 to 1984 African-Americans lost 56,000 students before graduation from high school. The drop-out rate is a clear indication of the frustration felt by students, their families, and educators.[4]

In the great classic, *The Invisible Man,* Ralph Ellison outlines how the African-American is ignored, disrespected, and treated as less than human across America.[5] Sociologists Ohlin and Cloward theorized about blocked opportunities and Merton underlined "the ends justify the means" as the major and ruling factor in the American dream.[6] Either the members of scavenger gangs have perceived their opportunities to be blocked or they were strained to the point of frustration and decided that in order to become successful they would use the territorial gang mode in becoming the ultimate corporate gang organization.

GANG EVOLUTION

The evolutionary process of gangsterism passes through the various socialization stages that key sociologists developed. Sutherland's theory of differential association is highly applicable to Detroit's gang evolution.

This study reveals that although scavengers may bring certain criminal characteristics to a gang, it is during the territorial stage that older, experienced gang members educate the new, younger members. Gang C-1 schooled its new members not only on gang rules, but on "how to perform various tasks, jobs and assignments for the gang." The territorial phase signifies that the gang has become serious about entering the mainstream of crime. It does not mean that a gang has arrived—or achieved the status of serious crime—but that it is entering the arena of serious, major criminal activities and attitudes.

94

Some critics in Detroit downplay the subject of gangs, but the economic plight of Detroit has left the inner city ripe for crime. High unemployment coupled with a high drop-out rate from schools leaves a large and willing pool of job seekers. The education factor means that, as Merton charged, the poorly educated and jobless youth still yearn for the riches of American society. Gangs S-9, C-1, and C-2 all indicated that neighborhood camaraderie meant very little and that violence was either a part of life or the use of violence was justified because of the ends produced. Shaw and McKay and Durkheim, basing their theories on the same foundations as did Merton, said that the poor neighborhoods and the socioeconomics signaled to residents that their chances of escaping urban plight were meager.

Scavenger Gangs

Membership into any scavenger group or gang is based on one common bond—desire. If one is rejected by everything and everyone in Detroit, the likelihood of finding others in a similar state is very high. When the home fails and the schools, churches, and the social welfare program miss, chances are a scavenger group is being formed. To dismiss this segment of the urban population, which has always existed, is to be either dishonest or naive. Many scavengers come together simply to survive from day to day. To the outside world they may appear to be gangs or crews, but to the participants, this is their family, their school, their church.

The curtailment of social programs has hit this group very hard. Not only are we looking at reduction of federal job programs, day care, Head Start, and other programs, but community centers, where many scavengers had historically "hung out," have also disappeared. Some critics have called Detroit's scavengers just kids hanging out, nothing organized. This study defines scavengers as a gang stage for inner-city youth. The scavenger stage is paramount to the evolution of gangs in Detroit. In early Chicago, the infamous 42ers were scavengers from Little Italy prior to the territorial stage that eventually led to their becoming a major organized criminal organization. In Detroit in the 1920s the Berstein Brothers joined Norman Purple as both groups emerged from

95

the scavenger stage into the serious territorial stage.

Scavengers are the entry-level applicants in the job markets of the underworld. Drugs changed the lives of inner-city youths who had been trapped victims of the depressed socioeconomics in Detroit. Drug business has meant a new life for many individuals who no longer had the job corps or special education programs. Scavengers see the drug business as the way out of poverty. One does not need a GED or other certificate of educational achievements; and past brushes with police may be a plus in the gang world where, best of all, financial rewards are immediate.

In an interview, one large scavengers gang answered the leadership and organization question.

> Yeah, we're a crew . . . it's about learning the game from the big fellas. All of us are the leaders, the bosses. If one of the big fellas notices our crew, then we all get paid. You never know when you might get chose by the big fellas. Some dudes go with [C-1] or [C-2]. It don't matter as long as you get chose. Anyway, our crew is getting known. When I first hooked up with [S-8], I was ten. You just learn how to roll at first. It's like lots of times you don't even get near the real action. But one of our old boys is rolling, so he'll put in the word for one of us. I can remember Jake's brother bought all of us some new Breaker jackets 'cause he used to be with our crew. We went to a steak restaurant, about fourteen of us and he paid for everything: jackets and big steak dinners and desserts. It was def!

Scavenger life is full of doubt, misery, and uncertainty. The lure of corporate life is the carrot that makes scavengers into gang members.

Territorial and Corporate Gang Transition

In the 1980s when gangs moved beyond the scavenger stage, they took on some aspects of power. During the territorial stage, gangs must physically take power and designate persons, items, something as theirs. One police official called the territorial process the "Dog and Fire Hydrant" period for the gang. The gangs that become successful must have staying power. In order to have staying power, the gang must become serious *and* organized. "No collective category, no class, no group of any kind in and of itself wields power or can use it. Another factor must be present: that of organization."[7]

The use of physical and psychological intimidation by corporate gangs that is unacceptable to most people of the traditional culture. One only need look closely to see the correlation. Corporate gangs C-1 and C-2 used their organizations to sell narcotics and keep competition out of their business zones. Protecting a sales area or feudal fiefdom is nothing new or radical in America. "Consistent with long-established policies, the various gangs attempted to create and maintain a monopoly over a particular territory. Invasion by a competing organization resulted in gang warfare. Murders were commonplace."[8] Drug-related violence in Detroit in the 1980s is no different from the gang warfare of the Capone era. Both scavengers and corporates accept violence as a part of doing business in Detroit.

The no-drug use rule of corporate gangs is a serious, mature, business-based rule. Scavengers are just having fun and are not ready to sacrifice their drug habit for themselves or for a corporate cause. Corporate members pursue their goals and will achieve them regardless of what sacrifices they may have to make or what they may have to do. All of the corporate gangs in this study indicated that they would use violence against anyone. The scavengers reported that they too would use force. However, it was apparent from the group interviews that corporate members had been schooled to believe that violence is a powerful tool to be used to get what they desired. The scavengers displayed an attitude that violence was sporadic and perversely fun at times. The scavengers were in the first stage of learning gang behavior. Territorial gangs demanded seriousness, power, and responsibility. The commercialization of the corporate stage demands a code of ethics. Although all three stages share different views, the perception gained from this study is that, for the very first time in modern U.S. history, African-Americans have moved into the mainstream of major crime. Corporate gangs in Detroit are part of organized crime in America.

DRUGS AND DRUG BUSINESS

While the debate continues as to whether gangs exist, one need only focus on the devastation of the inner city. With no jobs and too little education, the scourge of drugs has been a two-edged sword of destruction. Individuals, groups of friends, crews, and gang members all are consuming hard drugs daily. Drug usage by scavengers is normal. If youngsters are not using drugs, then they are trying to sell them. In the midst of the war on crime is the war on drugs, the war on poverty, and the war on illiteracy; the battles go on and on.

According to the 1982 television program, "Kids and Heroin," Detroit had 50,000 heroin junkies. As one drug counselor commented:

> We couldn't treat all the drug addicts if we wanted to today even if they all would come in. Crack has made this city a living hell. Crack addicts are growing (in number) daily and you would be surprised at who's on crack. If you included the (suburbs), you would really be knocked out. Let me tell you, drugs are everywhere, my friend.

The drug infusion has created a city full of fiefdoms. Drugs have caused the study of gangs to move beyond the problem of juvenile delinquency. One retired police official assessed the problem from the perspective of law enforcement:

> It's like feudal China, there are pockets of entrenched drug operations all over the city. War on Drugs? We've lost that war, because we didn't have a battle plan. The young punks think they've won and they're flaunting it in our faces. You have warlords over little areas that control their little fiefdoms. There are young people acting as contractors for these warlords. They're out there bidding and competing for jobs to sell dope, deliver narcotics, or worse, to murder for money. Hell, the public is scared to death. I can understand it. I don't like it, but we as law enforcement officials can't protect the public always. The damn drug business is bigger than we like to admit. Kids and adults see the warlords spreading money and fame. They want some of that money. Soon as we put away one bunch, another one takes its place. Then you got professional people, like lawyers, giving these punks their service. It's making me want to cry. Dope has made these characters think they're rich and powerful!

The drug invasion in Detroit is part of a deadly foe that is sweeping the nation. The legitimate employment void is quietly being filled by the underground drug economy. Drugs have given juvenile gangs the money and power needed to grow and compete in the big leagues. On the West Coast, the number of youth gangs in Los Angeles has quadrupled from 15,000 in 1977 to 60,000 in 1987.[9] The microwave effect of the gang explosion is based on the megapowered drug business. The proliferation of drugs, money, and violence in Los Angeles is identical to the increase of drugs, money, and violence in Detroit. The business of drugs produces fast and easy money, and the latest sensation is the hot commodity, cocaine, and its derivative, crack.[10]

Detroit had been well-saturated with drug trading since the early 1970s. The reemergence of the deadly drug heroin was started in the later months of 1979 by an adult-led youth gang. This gang was to have a dramatic impact on Detroit and its youth. After the deadly harvest of heroin, the switch to cocaine and crack brought Detroit and its youngsters into major crime, unlike anything ever known in American history. Although comparison to the Prohibition era is obvious, cocaine and crack cocaine have provided goals, jobs, and economic realities that the African-American communities in Detroit had never seen before.

Cocaine is patently the most serious drug problem and, thus, the most serious youth problem of the 1980s.[11] Street level purity more than doubled, from about 28 percent in 1981 to approximately 58 percent in 1986, while prices declined from $126/gram in 1981 to $80/gram in 1986.[12] Initially, it was thought that cocaine was only for the rich and that it was nonaddictive. But we know now that cocaine is *addictive and that its derivative, crack,* is extremely *addictive—and it is affordable.*

DRUGS AS EMPLOYMENT

When Gangs C-1 and C-2 were organized, it was almost impossible for scavengers to acquire the capital needed to invest in the drug ventures in Detroit. In 1982 Detroit had an estimated 50,000 heroin addicts,[13] but heroin has been the "other" drug since crack arrived. Crack is king in Detroit in 1989. Cocaine has its highest popularity with young people.[14] A more serious consequence of this endemic utilization has been the inclusion of more youngsters in the business of drug distribution at the street level.[15]

Corporate gangs laid the foundation of using juveniles for drug distributions in the inner city of Detroit. Drugs have given scavenger gangs hope for the future. As one scavenger stated:

> *I didn't do shit in school, my people ain't got no paper. I tried to join the Marines, I couldn't pass their written test. Ain't got no transportation to get a job. So what's a fella to do? You talk all that righteous shit, but you got a job. Got one for me? So I'm going to get with somebody rolling. . . . That's the only job for fellas like me.*

The Report of the Detroit Strategic Planning Project, focused on the depressing situation faced by Detroit's children.

> *Looking at a hopelessly bleak future, without opportunity or a decent life, many of these children view education as a worthless dead end, and they drop out of school in staggering numbers. Forty-one percent of Detroit's high schoolers will never graduate; and statistics show that even those who graduate have little success in finding jobs—their education simply hasn't prepared them for the technical job market. The correlation between young adults, unemployment, and crime is undeniable.[16]*

Although the hopelessness is more apparent for the low achievers, many potentially talented youngsters experience doubt, hopelessness, and uncertainty—like those who were labeled losers early in life. In many poor families the feeling of hopelessness is transmitted to the children.

> *Without a viable way for a parent to make a living, Detroit's traditional and historic family structure has become strained to the breaking point. Many families are torn by divorce. Recent statistics seem to indicate many black men aren't marrying simply because they have no jobs and cannot support families above the poverty line. By 1980, more than 80 percent of black families with incomes under $4,000 were headed by single women. The children of poverty are growing up fatherless, lacking the nurturing and guidance that formerly was seen as every child's birthright.[17]*

Drugs have become the opportunity for many inner city residents. Materialism in Detroit, like the rest of the larger society, has captured the minds of both young and old. While legitimate America cringes at the mention of drugs, the underworld, the underclass, and the under-educated minorities have merged into an unholy alliance with drugs. When asked what is the most important part of life, Detroit street gangs unanimously rated *money* number one. Society's major institutions—the home, the school, and the church—have lost the influence they had in the past.

Errol Henderson, a doctoral candidate at the University of Michigan, gave a powerful speech on gang violence at a forum during a conference at Kellogg Conference Center at Michigan State University. Henderson said, "Young people have been taught in this society that money is success. We tell them to get educated to make money. So when they make money from 'rolling,' they're only doing what we say do: make money! The kids say I'm making money, so I don't need an education."[18]

One of the most intriguing byproducts of this project has been the recognition of the concept that gang members and their peers throughout the city regard the drug trade as business. The money, cars, and clothes are the perks or rewards of their labor. The nexus between the communities and the evolutionary stages of the gang process is, for many participants, money and power. Until early 1980, Detroit youth gangs were locked in the scavenger stage. As with other ethnic gangs, development during the territorial stage brought about *organization*. Without organizing there could be no real power or consistency.

There is a great need for more in-depth research to understand why the scavenger development stage is populated by traditional problems of illiteracy, low self-esteem, and sporadic violence while at the same time youngsters from the same environment are assimilated into the corporate gang subculture. The evolution may be understandable for those downtrodden who have turned to outlaw ways. But the drug culture is affecting many middle-class and even some upper-middle-class youth who once said "no way" to crime.

Researchers have given valuable insights into this complex problem. In his speech, Errol Henderson correctly assessed the new era. "Never before in history have children twelve years old been able to make a living from selling drugs. Kids make more in one week than adults make in a month." Whether it's accepted or not, the fact remains as it did during prohibition, organized crime is business.[19]

THE QUISLING EFFECT

A quisling is one who works against his/her own nation, community, or people by siding with and/or assisting the invaders of that nation.

The community at large is the subculture in which urban gangs have thrived. Gang members constantly discussed involvement of the larger community. Over the course of this project it has become evident that some otherwise productive citizens are (1) indirectly involved with illegal business, (2) major consumers of illegal narcotics, (3) facilitating commerce with gang types involved in illicit matters, (4) involved directly in service and protection for individuals, groups, gangs from criminal prosecution, and (5) conducting legitimate businesses funded solely by illegally-made revenues.

There are businesses that covertly cater to gang types. The absence of a thriving economy haunts Detroit. The quisling culture manifested itself during the decline of a solid legitimate economy. During a heated interview, one real estate agent disputed objections to doing business with the young gangsters:

> If I don't sell houses to them, are you going to buy the houses? Hell, I'm in business, I don't ask people where their money comes from. Why don't you try selling property in this part of town. Or have you noticed? There are NO people on this street, NO stores worth mentioning, it's damn near impossible selling anything in this neighborhood. So, if someone wants to buy property I'm selling, okay? What am I supposed to do? Call the FBI, the police?

> First, sometimes you don't know who's buying what. Sometimes it's an older woman, a young girl. I've had white people, Arab people seeking property. Later, you see it's something else going on. But that is NOT my business, the

property is sold. I don't want to know what anybody does, okay? If they got the financing that's all the better. I'm just trying to make a living. I pay my taxes, work every day and try to keep my family fed and clothed. I don't break any laws, I don't sell drugs, and I don't use drugs. If these kids want to buy my properties, I'm not the police. I sell houses, that's my livelihood, okay? Anyway, why pick on the little dumb gang boys, it's the big rich dealers you never see. Probably 'cause they're the people controlling taxes and the world.

Instead of giving to society, quisling motivation is to take from society. Drug trade has escalated into a billion-dollar industry. Detroiters are victims of traitors who give nothing to the community. It is even more despicable when the outlaws and their collaborators have committed their acts of treachery, then blame the victims for the problems of decaying urban life. In some cases, it was very clear who the quislings were. Yet, there have to be others who are entrenched, and unknown. Gangs were conducting commerce that produced $7.5 million weekly. This in itself suggested that the quisling culture goes beyond the inner-city youth and Detroit.

In a broad sense, quislings have always existed in America. Organized crime has preyed on the public for years. The proliferation of drug money in the inner city of Detroit has eroded the traditional values. Illegal business is the reason for impoverished youngsters. There is no acceptable rationale for the clothier, car dealer, banker, or politician whose reasoning is guided by simple greed. As this project progressed, the quisling culture became more visible. The reckless violence of drug gangs is repugnant to the public. Yet, the recreational drug consumer, and the business person who prospers from intermixing with drug traders are no different from violent gang members.

GANG SUBCULTURE

Walter Miller, the noted researcher, implied that lower-class individuals have their own values and are not necessarily rejecting middle-class values. Miller also states that lower-class families are usually headed by females. Miller contends

103

that America has a large number of poor people who are economically depressed and isolated.[20]

This study of gangs supports Miller's conclusions about female-based, poverty-stricken homes. Some gang members in this study were establishing a set of rules in an outlaw culture that were different from traditional African-American values. Some of the scavenger gangs and their families interviewed in this study showed ignorance, resentment, and hostility. However, some gang members shifted their rationalization of criminal behavior from immorality to amorality. In Detroit scavenger gang members did not concern themselves with right or wrong. They relished machismo and toughness, and they were willing to physically prove their worth.

In the case of scavengers, status in a gang may be perceived as the only path to success. They have usually failed in school, at home, and in other social institutions. Many youngsters replace their birth families with gang families. In some cases, gang leaders were fulfilling the role of surrogate parents. When all other avenues have failed, gangs provide the only family some youngsters feel they have. Some gang members feel that the primary purpose of belonging to a gang is to cause problems in society.

Corporate gangs clearly understand that business is their first priority. They simply cannot understand casual fun, pranks, or overt acts of violence. Some corporate members regard scavengers as second-class citizens in the world of crime. Miller suggests that lower-class culture rejects middle-class culture. This study found, however, that some scavengers were looking for a way out of their subculture. In general, scavengers identified with a great deal of the middle-class African-American values and culture. Material items—houses, cars, and high-priced clothing—were important. Many scavengers think it is okay to take what they want from middle-class America (items such as fancy clothing, money, and power), from corporate gangs (status, notoriety, fame, money, and purchasing power), or from African-Americans (family structure and professional status).

One gang member said, "Cosby got the def family, fine wife, cool kids . . . but sometimes he should get more fly with his pieces (clothes)." Indirectly scavengers express envy of nuclear families. Although they reject the rules of middle-class society and, in most cases, middle-class controls, they do not reject the material rewards of middle-class life. Both scavenger and corporate gangs, when given the opportunity, have copied the lifestyles of middle- and upper-class America.

Gerald Ward, a part-time recreational aide and part-time drug courier for a gang of scavengers moving into the territorial stage, explains why he reads the *Robb Report:* "They've got all the information on bad rides, boats, watches, diamonds, and . . . *[we know]* all the mugs that are rolling buy their shit from places that advertise in the *Robb Report.* It messes with people's minds when they check me out reading the *Robb Report* . . . shows I got class."

Vincent Piersante has outlined the process for gang success not only in Detroit but anywhere. "With money comes power . . . power to move and gain more power, perhaps political power." Organized crime has used that formula for years. Detroit gangs have just now entered the power arena.[21]

Business or War?

The savagery of drug commerce has many observers concerned. The ruthlessness of Detroit gangs is not new or isolated. The homicide rate in Detroit has been infamous since the early 1970s. However, drug enterprising is inter-city, inter-state, intra-state, and international. Illegal commodities, whether drugs or alcohol, have always exposed the public to danger as criminals seek to carry on with their deadly trade.

Detroit has been called a war zone, and without question it is a war zone. But it is only a business zone for young outlaws, war lords, and illegal narcotic networks. The subculture of gang life in Detroit is growing. Corporate gangs have mesmerized the scavengers and used that as a source of its power. This study declares that the lifestyle of corporate gangs has the internal power to control its own organization; dictates external power to intimidate the innocent and tantalize the weak; and is strong enough to control a major business in the corporate sense of American capitalism.

John Kenneth Galbraith, in *The Anatomy of Power,* states, "The Mafia and other criminal organizations gain external power by the threat or reality of condign power. And this is also used internally to ensure the submission of their own members."[22]

There is nothing romantic, adventurous, or even honorable about Detroit's gangs. The reality is ugly, painful, and embarrassing. The criminal commerce of drugs includes armed robbery, break-ins, prostitution, and gangland-style murders.[23] The evolution of gangs has been enhanced by the illegal narcotics industry. Crime is the only choice many youngsters feel can pay off successfully in the long run. Is it business, or is it war? It's both—the individuals in the gangs are working. Combat and warfare are part of their job. The fact that their business is part of society's "War on Drugs," "War on Crime," "War on Poverty," and the other battles of social injustice and economic disparity is irrelevant in their world.

War is defined in the *Random House Dictionary* as "(a) a conflict carried on by force of arms, as between two nations or between parties within a nation; (b) aggressive business conflict, as through severe price cutting in the same industry or any other means of undermining competitors; (c) to be in conflict or a state of strong opposition; (d) to carry on active hostility or contention." In relation to this study, gangs are very much involved in war.

Detroit, like other urban environments is at war and in war. Conflict is being carried out through armed force between parties within the city. Individuals, groups, and gangs who are employed in the illegal narcotics business are in direct conflict. Rival parties are in conflict over business dealings. The wars overlap boundaries.

The war in Detroit also pits law enforcement agencies against the armies of organized crime via corporate gangs and scattered guerrilla forces of scavenger gangs. Their crimes against innocent citizens drastically reduce the quality of life in many neighborhoods. The powerful forces of corporate gangs are very aggressive during business conflicts. Gangs have used price slashing marketing practices in selling their product (i.e., drugs) to the public. They also have used physical intimidation and deadly force to sell their product. Gangland war is instrumental in undermining the competition. Detroit gangs, like many other urban criminal organizations, wage "war" in their pursuit of the American dream. They have discovered that the profits from trafficking in illegal substances were worth going to war with not only with law enforcement officials, but with anyone who might stand in their organizations' path.

The "War on Poverty" is a perpetual state of conflict for those who are socially and economically trapped in the underclass. The welfare rolls are the "Selective Service" for potential gang members of both the scavenger and territorial groups with final graduation to the corporate stage. Those forgotten, neglected, and ignored people have transmitted their disgusted, disillusioned, and hopeless attitudes to their children. Those children believed the negative teachings. Interviews with youngsters involved with scavenger operations displayed strong opposition to anyone and everything unlike themselves or their impoverished environment.

The scavenger gangs often caused conflict, contention, and hostility, letting everyone know "We're here, unloved, forgotten, ignorant, hostile, and ready to cause trouble at any time." A young scavenger remarked, "I hate it when I see people walking around happy. They look at me like I'm nothing. . . . Me and my crew like to fuck with the niggahs that think they're white. If I see somebody and they look at me like I'm nothing, I look at them and let them know I might beast on them right NOW!" Hungry, angry, and confused, many youngsters join the army of scavengers.

Subculture Mores

The drug business that causes some inner-city neighborhoods to resemble war zones is certainly not confined to the inner city. Neighborhoods and suburbs both inside and outside the city limits are being deeply and adversely affected by the drug business. The fact that corporate gangs are selling millions of dollars worth of drugs each week is significant on two points: (1) inner-city and suburban residents are purchasing millions of dollars worth of drugs, and (2) despite a depressed (legal) economy, the illegal underground is vibrant and healthy. Despite the severely polarized city and its suburbs, communications are open between groups when it comes to illegal narcotics.[24]

Interviews with youngsters and adults in this study revealed that many inner city residents have become desensitized to the violence of the various crime and drug wars. The battles are psychological as well as physical. In Greater Detroit, invisible lines have been drawn that effectively separate the races and socioeconomic classes. Some children in the inner city have no dreams, no expectations. No one expects anything from them, and they in return expect nothing from themselves. A young teacher said, "When I first started teaching I expected something from my students. Now I expect nothing, and I'm never surprised that some parents and students don't expect anything."

In an interview with the *Detroit News*, University of Michigan professor Hazel Markus discussed her research on delinquent youth. The delinquents expected negative experiences, failure, and trouble.[25] "Of the delinquent kids, 65 percent said no one or nothing influenced them in the last year."[26] The general consensus of scavengers and corporates is that of detachment and autonomy. This total separation from mainstream values, concerns, and rules signals that gang members belong to another culture.

The high school dropouts who joined scavenger communes throughout the city are divided in their search for identity. Rev. Keith Butler, a church and community leader, said of young gang members: "Their self-image is poor . . . need better role models." But outsiders could make a grave error by assuming that all scavenger and other gang members have low self-esteem.

Gaylord Washington, a former community youth worker, offers:

> The little gangs, the knucklehead boys in our neighborhood, are just kids lost with no jobs, no good parents and nobody who gives a damn. The community centers closed when Reagan took over. . . . People used to say things like, "We don't need no community center. Young punks just play basketball and hang around doing nothing." But we used to have community centers all over this city. They helped, kids could find something to do and we used to hire kids for jobs. There was hope, people

need hope. Now everybody is in the streets, good kids, bad kids . . . everybody is out in the streets. Survival is the only game these kids can play.

The universal rule of neither talking to nor cooperating with police authorities can be traced back to biblical days. Corporate gangs utilized infrastructures that resemble paramilitary and Mafia organizations. The gang subculture has its own rules: street law controls the behavior of these gangs. The gangs in this study were part of a very active and cohesive subculture. They police themselves, as did earlier ethnic criminal organizations.

Some of the basic codes of conduct followed in youth and adult gangs are quite similar. A universal requirement is loyalty to the group. Providing information to the authorities is considered an unpardonable sin. In youth gangs "squealing" may be punished by inflicting a severe beating of the offender or in extreme cases marking him for death. In adult organized crime groups, those suspected of talking to officials are executed. Frequently they are unmercifully tortured before being killed.[27]

Females and Gangs

An interesting byproduct of this study was the awareness of the involvement of young girls and women in the gang world. The study was unable to focus the resources or attention that this new phenomenon demands, however, there is no doubt that women are very involved in gang activities. Historically, young women and female juveniles have been relegated to peripheral and ambiguous positions. Thrasher's classic, *The Gang*, barely mentioned females in neighborhood gangs.[28] Over the years, Detroit gangs displayed the usual male-female relationship in the evolutionary process. Those relationships were mainly two-pronged: (1) friendship—as girlfriend-boyfriend, or as friends, buddies, or pals; and (2) relatives—such as sisters, brothers, cousins, aunts, or uncles.

In Malcolm W. Klein's book, *Street Gangs and Street Workers*, findings regarding female delinquency and gangs paralleled the findings of this study. "Evidence from an independent [study shows that] girls' groups usually consist at

109

first of sisters and girl friends of male gang members, but that they have soon taken on a more diverse membership as the girls recruit new members among their own friends."[29] It is not new for girls to be working in the auxiliary mode. In a *Ms.* magazine article about East Los Angeles gangs, Suzanne Murphy described typical scavenger characteristics. Most of the female members who were affiliated with a male gang usually played the traditional roles of girlfriends or weapon carriers.[30]

The present study identified traditional auxiliary relations between Detroit females and male gang members. Attitudes of independence, aggressiveness, and equality have created a new wave of female gangs. The characteristic definition for females is no different from that of males.

In this study the researcher acknowledges that female and male gangs, crews, or groups are not always negative or threatening to the public. But when the gang is involved in criminal behavior, society needs to become concerned. Females are not exempt from the process of scavenger-territorial-corporate stages. They have already participated in the various stages as auxiliary members, friends, or relatives. The small female crew we interviewed was in transition from the scavenger to the territorial stage. We found no female gangs that had independently entered the corporate stage, however, it is reasonable to suppose that in time females will graduate to corporate status. The female gang attitudes were interwoven with those of other urban youngsters expressing the desire for money, material items, and status. Detroit female gang members were not conscious of women's liberation.

Although females were not part of the major crime wave in Detroit, this new attitude bears close scrutiny. Of the females surveyed, 87 percent (three-fourths were non-gang females) acknowledged carrying some type of weapon. In interviews, non-gang females openly socialized with, and in many cases condoned the behavior of, gang members, especially corporate gang members. Females, whether involved with a gang or neutral, were aware of their position in the community. Like the other youngsters in this study, females wanted power, status, and respect from society. There was no dichotomy of "good girls" vs. "bad girls." This was never more evident than when non-gang females were asked if they would socialize with gang members. The majority answered that they would socialize and that their parents would not object. The interconnecting thread between the sexes and classes was money.

CONCLUSION

To date, this separate gang subculture has not been studied, much less acknowledged. The complex, intricate, and foreign (to the American mainstream) environment is well entrenched. The roots of this subculture can be traced back to the early days of slavery. Herman and Julia Siegel Schwendinger, in their book *Adolescent Subcultures and Delinquency,* scrutinized economic conditions and the parallel between delinquents and their peer support.[31]

This support of peers is similar to the building of a separate society for youngsters in urban America.

In his book, *Delinquent Boys,* Albert Cohen contended that middle-class values are the measuring rod for all of society's children.[32] Many of the youngsters in this study have not only rejected those ruling standards, but have replaced them with their own value system. In that rejection, both scavengers and corporate gangs have created their own societies. Like foreign ruffians invading a village, these juveniles are pillaging the town treasures and pursuing materialism. They are not interested in African-American or American history or contemporary issues. Many of these juveniles and their families have been oppressed, neglected, and ignored. Some of their perspectives are hostile, malicious, and perverted. More knowledgeable gang members believe most Americans are engaging in illegal activities, and that they are hypocrites.

This study concluded that Detroit youth in the 1980s are drawn to gangs for the following reasons: (1) jobs that make big money, (2) solidarity of identification with a group, which ensures protection from rivals, outsiders, or other threatening individuals, (3) status or a sense of belonging, (4) a sense of camaraderie among peers, and (5) adventure.

111

Further research in the area of urban gangs is urgently needed. The various theorists mentioned in this study have laid solid groundwork on which we were able to build. Yet, this is definitely a new era in the urban environments of America. Though this study of Detroit gangs supports previous studies of gangs and juveniles, contemporary issues such as drugs, weaponry, technology, sexuality, and socioeconomics have not been adequately studied. Drugs have been the super-agents of change. Drugs are not only a dilemma from the perspective of consumption, but also as a vehicle for economic gain. Cocaine has become the "atomic bomb" as convicted Colombian cocaine kingpin Carlos Lehder called it during an interview.[33] Detroit urban gangs are using drugs as their vehicle for social mobility.

When this study was started, drug trade in Detroit was built on heroin, from which corporate gangs made millions of dollars. By 1984, cocaine had replaced heroin and Gang C-1 had become history. After its demise, other gangs copying C-1's style and management continued the lucrative drug trade. Despite winning battles, law enforcement is losing the war on drugs. Urban youth gangs are very much part of this war. This study has opened the door to a separate society that is growing daily and spreading throughout America. Young gang members have proved that their proficient dramaturgy has tricked America. There is much that America does not understand, much less accept, about this dangerous society.

A street-wise former gambler and pimp offered this assessment of youth gangs in Detroit:

> These young boys are different. Everything is different today—food, cars, women, men, people call you black then African, colored, and I remember negro. But these kids are crazy. They're ready to kill anybody. They'll kill their mommas, friends, police, or themselves. When we were coming up, sporting people didn't mingle with dope people. Now almost everybody is dope people. These kids have grown up too damn fast, seen too much wrong . . . plus they ain't got nothing for these young boys to do. Pimping is dead, you can't get no good clean sex, 'cause all the girls is doped up. Now, in my day we didn't let our stables fool around with hoppers, no sir. We used to keep kids away from the fast life. Sure, we weren't church people, but we respected other

folks. These gangs are deadly. They'll hurt little kids, women, 'cause they don't abide by rules of anybody. We had rules, and we knew we were to have our business. But mainly these boys are violent and mad. They get money and they're still shooting up folks. I'm glad that I'm old and had my day.

Today, these youngsters are walking around laughing and shooting up anybody they feel like. People better wake up and deal with these boys or they going to take over the whole town.

Notes

1. Merton, "Social Structure and Anomie."
2. *Report of the Detroit Strategic Planning Committee.*
3. Ibid.
4. Ibid.
5. Ralph Ellison, *Invisible Man* (New York: Random House, 1947).
6. Lloyd Ohlin and Richard Cloward, *Delinquency and Opportunity: A Theory of Delinquent Gangs* (New York: The Free Press of Glencoe,m 1960).
7. *Report of the Detroit Strategic Planning Committee.*
8. Ibid.
9. "The Hollow Promise," *U.S. News & World Report*, 7 November 1988, 41-44.
10. "Kids & Cocaine," *Newsweek*, 17 March 1986, 58-65, quoting the Comptroller General of the United States (GAD Publishing, 1987, 1988), and the Washington D.C. "Drug Abuse Status Report."
11. Maureen A. Mickalonis, "Evaluating Alternatives for Juvenile Offenders" (December 1988, unpublished).
12. Comptroller General of the United States, "Controlling Drug Abuse: A Status Report," 1988.
13. "Kids and Heroine," WXYZ-TV, Southfield, Michigan, December 1984.
14. "Kids and Cocaine," *Newsweek*.
15. Ibid.
16. *Report of the Detroit Strategic Planning Committee.*
17. Ibid.
18. Errol Henderson, speech given at the Governor's Conference on Violent Youth Offenders, Kellogg Conference Center, Michigan State University, East Lansing, 7 December 1988.
19. Ibid.
20. Walter Miller, "Lower Class Culture as a Generating Milieu of Gang Delinquency," *Journal of Social Issues* 14, no. 3 (1958).

21. Vincent Piersante, interview, 14 May 1987.

22. John Kenneth Galbraith, *The Anatomy of Power* (Boston: Houghton Mifflin Co., 1983).

23. *Report of the Detroit Strategic Planning Committee.*

24. Ibid.

25. Hazel Markus, *Detroit News*, 1 January 1989, 1-A.

26. Ibid.

27. *Report of the Detroit Strategic Planning Committee.*

28. Thrasher.

29. Malcolm W. Klein, *Street Gangs and Street Workers* (Englewood Cliffs, N.J.: Prentice-Hall, Inc., 1971).

30. Suzanne Murphy, "1978: A Year with the Gangs of East Los Angeles," *Ms.*, 7 (July), 56-64.

31. Herman Schwendinger and Julia Siegel Schwendinger, *Adolescent Subcultures and Delinquency* (NY: Praeger, 1985).

32. Albert Cohen, *Delinquent Boys. The Culture of the Gang* (Glencoe, Ill.: The Free Press, 1955).

33. Carlos Lehder quoted in an interview in "Getting Tough on Cocaine," *Newsweek*, November 1988: 76.

COMMUNITY TEAM EFFORT

American cities are wrestling with the social changes of the 1980s. Industrial centers have been hardest hit by the demise of heavy industries such as automobile manufacturing. The devastation caused by these declining markets has left cities like Detroit depressed. The loss of jobs, especially those that had existed for the past seventy years, was also the loss of a way of life.

The realities of economic depression have caused a ripple effect through the middle class, into the working class, lower class and underclass. Welfare rolls have swollen as many of the temporary lay-offs experienced by urban residents have translated into permanent job losses. When the loss of jobs paralyzes economic growth, taxes shrink and community services are reduced. In truth, community services were usually already strained in cities such as Washington, D.C., Chicago, New York, or Detroit. Adequate resources were simply not available to meet the increased social and economic needs brought about by the upheaval of the 1970s and 1980s.

Many of these same cities were victims of civil riots during the late 1960s and early 1970s. Detroit, for example, was the site of the worst civil riot in the history of America. Newark, Los Angeles, and New York experienced similar riots which gutted the inner cities of their vital organs. Those organs were the church, neighborhood movie theaters, drugstores, supermarkets, cleaners, hardware stores, clothing stores, restaurants, etc. As each neighborhood business was lost, so were those jobs it supported. The worst loss of all however, was the spirit of the community—loss of continuity, friendship, neighborhood bonds, and familiarity. As social controls were vitiated, people felt isolated and lost.

The knowledge of gang violence, not only in warfare but on anyone who might threaten their interest, has muzzled many citizens. The researchers found the attitudes of gang members to be very callous and insensitive toward the public. America has found that, as in the Prohibition era, today's drug traffickers are completely unconcerned about the public's safety. It is apparent that the community at large has to come together to combat this deadly foe. The following strategies address the situation.

What is needed is a Community Team Effort (CTE) to deal with gang-related criminal activities. The community team effort consists of the following: (1) the family and the home, (2) strong schools, (3) jobs, the economy, and the role of businesses, (4) criminal justice, and (5) the church.

Ideally, the best strategy for any community to pursue is prevention. Preventing drugs from getting an anchor in the community is the best offensive for the community team effort. Drug education at home, in our schools, in the churches, at our businesses, workplaces and in government, in all aspects of our daily life, would stop the drug dealers internationally and domestically. However, at present the reality is that drugs are as American as hot dogs, baseball, and apple pie.

STRATEGY 1: THE FAMILY AND THE HOME

Home is where children should learn that drugs are taboo. Poor examples by adults on the home front erode the role modeling of drug-free adults. Parents must be explicit in their aggressive rejection of *all* drugs; such as the young single mother who had sincerely impressed upon her young son that her expectation of him was to stay drug-free. She had let it be known in no uncertain terms: NO DRUGS! A strong home combats drugs for potential users or sellers.

In an interview on public television, Arthur Ashe, the tennis great, acknowledged that his father's expectations of him were high. Ashe insisted that he couldn't hurt his father by performing any negative deeds. His final comments regarding his father's discipline were as follows: "If I messed up, got in trouble, I knew he would kick my ass."

The fact is that strong homes, whether in the ghettos of New York or in rural North Dakota, form the basis for combating the gang-drug menace. Single families— Italian, African-American, Polish-American—all have battled problems of poverty, discrimination, and crime. The home, supported by the extended family, neighborhoods, and businesses, molds children who can cope with the material- istic lure of drug gangs. The family is the nucleus in mobilizing the community. Strong families are the foun- dation of good neighborhoods. No matter what the family lacks, the void should be filled by the CTE through one of the other units, i.e., church, school, social worker, or neighbors.

STRATEGY 2: STRONG SCHOOLS

Strong schools that refuse to allow drugs or drug- related activities of any sort in the school environment are needed. Prevention at the school yard is paramount. Comprehensive teaching of the whole school should address those students from troubled homes. Students should be educated about ethics, human welfare, and their neighborhoods, and they should be taught that drugs are negative for consumers—and worse for those selling them.

No signs of gold chains, cars, clothes, or any suggestions of drug-trade symbols of success should be allowed. If necessary, students should wear uniforms. The business community, the neighborhoods, or the community at large might underwrite uniform expense if necessary. Children must learn that drug involvement is negative—against everything and everybody.

117

Communities must be encouraged to utilize schools as extensions of the home. Schools should be open after regular hours. Activities that give youngsters something to do everyday should take place at the school. Juvenile authorities should send delinquents to school with assignments that counteract juvenile transgressions. Activities should focus on academics, cultural activities, sports, and current local, state, national, and international subjects. Professionals who can serve as role models should donate their services by making one-year commitments. Schools must become the central point for youth when they are away from home. Schools and the community must focus on troubled students and delinquents, perhaps tracking them into special units with intensive help from teachers, counselors, and special parent-substitutes. Troubled students cannot be ignored. Some communities have magnet schools for able students, but without intervention the students from poor backgrounds are more than likely to become gang members involved in drug business. Drugs, especially as they relate to schools, must be stopped.

Searches of student lockers, given "reason to suspect," may be needed in certain communities. At some schools constant surveillance for drugs and weaponry may be needed. Neighbors and the total community should be eyes and ears looking for any gang-related drug distribution. Starting with preschool children, drug education is necessary in today's world. Schools should serve as the beacon for the community. Parents must demand drug-free schools. Teachers and staff must be on the lookout for activities that are suggestive of drug trade and use. Strong homes and schools can be major forces in eliminating gang and drug problems.

Schools must be allies of the criminal justice system. Police, not teachers, are the law enforcers, and that relationship must be clear and solid. The strong school communicates with others in the CTE. The business of educating can ill afford to have drugs or gangs as the inspiration and center of attention of any educational institution.

An increasing number of school systems are proving that all children can learn and experience success in school.

James P. Comer, writing in *Scientific American,* November 1988, explained how schools can successfully educate poor minority children. To quote from Comer,

> *The task seems overwhelming. And yet it can be done. In 1968 my colleagues and I at Yale University's Child Study Center started an intervention program at two inner-city schools in New Haven. Unlike many of the reforms that are now being tried or proposed, which focus on academic concerns such as teacher credentials and basic skills, our program promotes development and learning by building supportive bonds that draw together children, parents, and school. By 1980 academic performance at the two New Haven schools had surpassed the national average, and truancy and disciplinary problems had declined markedly. We have now begun to duplicate that success at more than 50 schools around the country.*[1]

Prince George's County (Maryland) Public Schools, with 103,000 students and Norfolk (Virginia) Public Schools with 36,000 students have achieved notable success in educating poor, minority students. All but 10 percent of the students in Prince George's County came from low-income homes. Students who once scored far below the norm now score above the 90th percentile on achievement tests. In Norfolk, a transient community near a naval base, students, 56 percent of whom come from the lower socioeconomic stratum, have made similar gains. Why? School improvement efforts based on Comer's concepts and Effective Schools Research have provided solid principles on which to base change. With the dual goal of quality and equity that these two school systems used as their credo, all children can learn, regardless of race, gender, or socioeconomic status. This outlook is an important part of making a difference. The seven conditions or correlates taken from Effective Schools Research are: a clear and focused school mission, high expectations for achievement of all children, safe and orderly school environment, strong instructional leadership, frequent monitoring of student progress, opportunity to learn and time on task, and good home-school relations.

Schools in virtually every state in the union are making needed changes as part of a school improvement process.

Parents are a very important part of this process. Some districts that have shown their determination to be accountable for the academic progress of students are gaining strong financial support in their communities.

STRATEGY 3: JOBS, THE ECONOMY, AND THE ROLE OF BUSINESS

Jobs play a significant role in combating gangs and drugs. The neglect of inner-city youth employment has been exacerbated by the desire of youth to obtain material treasures. The value of simple minimum-wage jobs for youngsters has been forgotten. When drug distributing becomes the employer, $3.65 or $8.65 can't compete with drug business income.

Juveniles and adults in neighborhoods that have respectable jobs for them before drugs enter the picture are capable of saying "no." The education and school strategy must prepare the family and neighborhood to decide against spending their respective wages for drug consumption or investment. (Some communities have experienced legitimate wages being invested in drugs for sale in the community. Instead of investing in the stock market or banks, some citizens are using gang-related drug organizations as their banking institution.)

The private sector must assist in developing jobs for the communities. The work ethic has eroded in recent years. Neighborhoods need services and residents should be part of that first-line business. Neighborhood stores must employ local youth and adults so that people feel part of the community. Respectable jobs, strong homes, and good schools in a caring and positive community can help keep youngsters from being misguided. Teens must understand the importance of working and building neighborhoods. National advertising could assist communities by presenting positive advertising about respectable jobs vs. unrespectable jobs such as gang-related drug trade. Jobs can keep youngsters busy and away from destructive behavior. The community should prepare children for moving through levels of job responsibility. Cleaning up the environment, fixing abandoned homes, working with senior citizens—there are numerous jobs that the government, the private sector, churches, and schools could support in some manner, perhaps on a permanent basis. The old adage of teaching a man to fish, which will enable him to provide for himself, rather than giving him fish, is the key to this strategy.

STRATEGY 4: CRIMINAL JUSTICE

The main focus of this strategy is to control crime. Controlling drug traffic will reduce crime. No positive community can function in the midst of high crime.

Communities must have strong support from law enforcers, and law enforcers must have strong support from the community. Protection was the key concern of many local residents interviewed. Neighborhoods must be willing to uncover any drug-related activities. Drug consumers in the community or outsiders who come looking for drugs must find a united neighborhood that will not tolerate drugs under any conditions. When families and schools work together, the criminal justice system can be more effective in combating drug-related crime. Law enforcers must have witnesses who will identify drug traders and ways to protect those witnesses must be developed.

The police officers in the trenches must have public support. The first step is to disarm gang members and other individuals in the drug business. An aggressive attack on illegal firearms is essential. Drug traders should not have high-powered firearms. All illegal firearms should be confiscated and publicly destroyed. Citizens and law enforcers should have a moratorium period to allow all illegal firearms to be turned in without penalty, but after that moratorium, illegal guns used or found must be destroyed. Those found to still possess them should suffer grave consequences. There can be no middle ground, no compromise. Total disarmament of illegal weapons is the only viable way to begin securing any community.

The government should be able to confiscate the assets of gangs, their associates, and drug users. This is crucial.

Without the money they have no power. Illegally-obtained money should be confiscated, whether it is in the possession of juveniles or their parents. The respectable jobs strategy can't work or compete against drug jobs. Incarceration should be secondary to removal of assets.

The punishment of gang-related drug distribution is paramount in combating this complex problem. When the police remove gangs and the prosecutor's office successfully prosecutes and confiscates assets, the correctional system must begin the process of punishment, rehabilitation, education, and reevaluation of those guilty of drug trafficking.

Correctional facilities need to have personnel available to work with society's problems and not merely to babysit inmates. Verified reports confirm that gangs continue their drug operations from within prison walls. The question of civil rights of inmates creates problems for all involved, but the fact remains that drug distribution by gangs seldom if ever plays by fair rules, ethics, or with regard for community concern. Punishment is important in letting potential users as well as dealers know that they will face serious penalties for their transgressions.

Neighborhoods and leaders must demand that no one in the community become allied with drug distribution. Researchers have found hypocritical attitudes among many upstanding citizens who either use drugs or profit from drug money. Society must realize that law enforcement alone cannot solve this problem. Given the proper support, law enforcement is the key to dismantling gang-related drug operations. Taking away weapons and finances can help to solve the problem. If conditions in American cities do not change, the problem will certainly reappear. The CTE is only as potentially effective as society makes it.

STRATEGY 5: THE CHURCH

The church has a very crucial role to play in combating the drug problem. (Church means synagogue, parish, mosque, or any place of worship.) Historically, the church has been a sanctuary for individuals, offering refuge, assistance, and guidance to anyone in need. The researchers found that all gang types in this study had virtually no relationship to a church. Religion today has been caught in the negative light of TV evangelism scandals. Unfortunately, the public, youngsters included, see that some church leaders are not above everyday sin and certainly not above reproach.

The church can play a significant role in promoting family values, reinforcing home training, encouraging school attendance, school manners, better morals, and stronger ethics. Like all other social institutions in our society, the church has been challenged. Churches need to renew their efforts to promote lasting spiritual values and point out the pitfalls of materialism. Some churches may wish to support community activities during the week, such as bowling, basketball, choir, dances, and plays. Though church-sponsored activities might seem unimportant, such activities could help to create a constructive and positive community atmosphere. Gang-related drug distribution in a neighborhood with strong churches will have a much more difficult time carrying on drug operations.

The church provides the moral foundation of many communities. Clergymen must set the tone for adults and youth in the community. In a midwest city that was invaded by drug gangs, the church was the spearhead of a community coalition against the drug traders. A men's group took it upon themselves to stop wearing expensive gold jewelry. This simple act was to set the tone for the young men in the church and neighborhood. This example seems small, but the message was clear. In addition, the men of the church conducted marches and rallies, attended judicial proceedings, encouraged counseling for offenders, became involved in the support and rehabilitation of young persons, and sought help from local merchants to create a teen recreation center.

Churches must be committed to challenging youngsters to become involved in constructive endeavors. Churches, like schools, must be looking for ways to help those in need. For some, the church could become a home away from home. Church activities could include education, day care, and other community-oriented activities. The role of the church, as with other components of the CTE, will be defined according to local needs. The important point is that they be pro-active.

The CTE needs to be flexible in attacking gang-related drug distribution. Society can ill afford to turn away or ignore the problem as if it belonged to someone else. Parents need support from the church, school, police, mayor, and the community in general. In an interview, Ron Shigur, assistant prosecutor for juveniles in Wayne County, indicated that traditional juvenile delinquents need to be separated from the new breed of hard-core delinquents who require intensive counseling and well-supervised probation. Communities need to address genuine rehabilitation of delinquents. Volunteers in some communities have developed meaningful one-on-one relationships that have facilitated lasting changes in persons who were formerly delinquent. People must remember that, if ignored, delinquency and crime will only multiply. Gangs get their members from throw-away children. The community team must be there to ensure that no children are forgotten, much less thrown away. The complete community, including individuals in the neighborhoods, must take a stand and be pro-active.

Gangs prey on weakness, indecisiveness, selfishness, and greed. Americans must not only say "Not in my neighborhood," but also say "Not in anyone's neighborhood, either." We can no longer tolerate "us" versus "them" attitudes. Drug consumers must be punished; dealers must be punished. Some highly organized gangs have gained support from too many segments of the community because of the power they have achieved through drugs, money, and guns. Do we want inaction, passivity, and fearfulness to determine our future?

The home is the starting point. Parents and guardians must teach young people that gangs, drugs, and money are not the solution to economic and social problems. Society must reinforce that message. Respectable jobs and good schools need the opportunity to function without the negative influences from drug-selling gangs. Police and courts must be able to do their jobs. The business community must invest time and money in order to preserve a healthy business climate. The responsibility of the community is to maintain the climate for effective, normal interaction among local residents. United communities can more effectively combat gang-related drug distribution than can those that are not. Refusing to allow the drug business to become entrenched is vital in defending communities. No one-step solution will combat drugs and gangs.

A 19-year-old gang member commented on the life of drug trafficking: "I'd probably be doing something if I wasn't rolling. But you know it's just part of life. You don't see nobody trying to stop us from selling dope? If people don't want it, they shouldn't buy it!"

NOTES
1. James P. Comer, "Educating Poor Minority Children," *Scientific American*, (November 1988) Vol. 259:42-48

APPENDICES

TABLE 1

Individual Interviews with Gang Members
1980–85

	Scavenger	Corporate

FAMILY INFORMATION

1. Do you live with:

Father and mother	0	6
Mother	29	15
Father	2	8
Live with grandparents	1	5
Live with brother/sister	3	6
Live with friends	5	0

2. Age of parents:

Under 35	13	11
Under 40	7	13
Under 45	4	5
No answer	16	11

3. Education you have completed:

Elementary	21	15
Middle school	5	23
High school	2	2
College	0	0
Hadn't finished any school	12	0

4. Parent(s) education:

Elementary	14	16
Middle school	9	13
High school	13	26
College	0	2

5. Do you have any children?

Yes	24	9
No	16	31

129

	Scavenger	Corporate

NEIGHBORHOOD INFORMATION

6. **Do you know your neighbors on your block/street?**

	Scavenger	Corporate
Yes	9	4
No	31	36

7. **Do you help your neighbors with problems in the community?**

Yes	2	0
No	38	40

8. **Are there businesses in your neighborhood (drug stores, grocery stores, clothing stores, auto parts, party/convenience stores, etc.)?**

Yes	6	6
No	34	34

9. **Is there a gun in your house?**

Yes	39	31
No	1	9

10. **Do you care about your neighborhood? (Example: Does it matter if there is a dope house on your street? Do you care if the house next door is vacant?)**

Yes	3	2
No	37	38

11. **Who controls crime in your neighborhood?**

Blacks	33	37
Arabs	7	2
Whites	0	1
Others	0	0

	Scavenger	Corporate

12. Who owns businesses in your neighborhood?

	Scavenger	Corporate
Blacks	4	17
Arabs	36	23
Whites	0	0
Others	0	0

PERSONAL INFORMATION

13. Do you have a job?

Yes	0	40
No	40	0

14. Do you want a job?

Yes	6	0
No	31	40
Don't know	3	0

15. Are you looking for a job?

Yes	6	0
No	34	0
N/A	0	40

16. Would you work a job for minimum wage?

Yes	0	0
No	37	40
No answer	3	0

17. Would you work a job that paid better than minimum wage?

Yes	39	21
No	14	0
No answer	3	5

18. Do you attend school?

Yes	4	28
No	36	2
Sometimes	10	0

	Scavenger	Corporate
19. When you or your gang commit any type of criminal act(s), do you plan them in advance?		
Yes	9	40
No	29	0
Don't know	2	0
20. Do you feel violence is part of everyday life?		
Yes	26	40
Don't know	4	0
No answer	10	0
21. How do your parents feel about your gang activities?		
Sanctioned OK	21	22
Didn't approve	9	7
OK if on rich people	8	0
Parents know something	0	8
Parents don't care	0	3
Parents don't care about anything	1	0
"I'm not with my parents anymore"	1	0
22. Do you use drugs, including alcohol?		
Yes	38	
No	2	

Scavengers	33 high use for alcohol
	38 high use for drugs

Corporate	40 no drugs
	22 alcohol on occasion
	12 alcohol every day
	3 no answer

23. Do you have any regrets about doing criminal acts?		
No	34	40
Don't know	3	0
No answer	3	0

132

	Scavenger	Corporate
24. Do you own a gun or have access to a gun?		
Yes	40	40
Own	14	37
Have access	3	0
25. Do you own a car?		
Yes	1	19
No	39	11
Scooter/motorcycle	0	10
26. Do you vote in elections?		
No	40	40
27. Who was Malcolm X?		
Knew	0	12
Didn't know	38	19
No answer	2	9
28. How do you feel about police?		
Like	0	8
Dislike	36	14
Neutral/doesn't matter	4	18
29. Are you close to your parents?		
Yes (Corporate 17 very, 20 medium)	2	37
No	24	13
No answer	14	7
30. How do you relate to whites?		
Like	0	5
Dislike	33	11
Don't care	6	24
No answer	1	0
31. Given the chance, would you go back to school and get a good job?		
Yes	21	3
No	10	37
No answer	9	0

133

	Scavenger	Corporate
32. Have you participated in illegal enterprises to make money?		
Yes	27	40
No	13	0
(38 Corporates indicated it was not illegal to them.)		
33. Have you sold drugs?		
Yes	19	33
No	0	7
No answer	21	0
34. Do you attend church?		
Yes	0	4
No	37	36
No answer	3	0
35. Do you date regularly?		
Yes	22	34
No	12	2
No answer	6	4
36. What is your favorite pastime?		
Sports	13	19
Gang activity	6	3
Nothing in particular	21	6
Other	0	12
37. Have you ever wanted to get out of the gang?		
Yes	13	2
No	11	34
No answer	16	4
38. Do you know of any professionals (teachers, ministers, lawyers accountants, business owners, etc.) who purchase illegal goods? (This question came from gang members commenting on "phony role-models, leaders, etc.")		
Yes	40	40

134

	Scavenger	Corporate
39. Do you know of any professional types who use drugs, alcohol, etc.?		
Yes	40	40
40. Do your parents use drugs, alcohol?		
Yes	39	16
No	1	24
41. Have you ever been arrested?		
Yes	30	8
No	3	32
No answer	7	0
42. How do you feel about prison as punishment?		
Concerned	0	6
Not concerned	40	0
Accepted punishment	0	14

TABLE 2
VIOLENCE
Group Interviews with Males
1980–1985

	Scavenger	Corporate
1. Have you ever seen someone shot or stabbed?		
Yes	20	20
No	0	0
2. Would your gang use violence against anyone?		
Yes	20	20
No	0	0
3. Have you or your gang committed any acts of violence?		
Yes	20	7
No answer	0	13
4. Are there times when violence is OK?		
Yes	12	20
No answer	8	0
5. What acts are OK for using violence?		
Self defense	12	14
When you want something	6	6
6. Have you or your gang ever been victims of violence?		
Yes	20	3
No	0	0
No answer	0	17
7. Would you or your gang use violence against anyone including authority figures such as the police?		
Yes	3	0
No answer	17	20
8. Did your parents ever use violence?		
Yes	16	2
No answer	4	18

	Scavenger	Corporate
9. Do you enjoy violence in movies and TV?		
Yes	20	8
No answer	0	12
10. If you think someone or something wrongs you, will you use violence to get even?		
Yes	20	20
No	0	0
11. What is the most important part of life?		
Happiness	0	0
Money	17	20
Clothes	0	0
Car	3	0
Good job	0	0
Friendship	0	0
Other	0	0

TABLE 3
Male Gang Members and Female Associates
1980–1987

	Scavenger	Corporate	Female
1. Have you ever seen the following amount of cash at one time (not in a bank or store?			
$ 1,000.00	40	40	32
5,000.00	40	40	19
10,000.00	40	40	19
15,000.00	32	40	14
20,000.00	26	31	14
25,000.00	21	29	14
More	18	23	14
2. Have you ever seen a (the actual weapon)?			
Uzi	40	40	32
MAC-10	40	40	32
.357 Magnum	40	40	32
Other	40	40	32
3. Do you know someone who owns the following?			
Mercedes Benz	40	40	32
BMW	40	40	32
Jeep Renegade	40	40	32
Cadillac	40	40	32
Other	40	40	32
4. Do you or someone you know own the following?			
Gucci	40	40	32
Louis Vuitton	40	40	32
Fila Sportswear	40	40	32
Adidas footwear	40	40	32

	Scavenger	Corporate	Female
5. Your favorite music is (may choose more than one)			
Jazz	0	0	0
Gospel	2	11	17
Rhythm and Blues	9	13	15
Pop	0	5	3
Country Western	0	0	0
Rap	40	40	32

TABLE 4

Hart Plaza, July 4, 1986

Investigators interviewed 25 youngsters at random in the concessions area: Subjects were selected based on three factors: (1) they didn't appear to be with any gang types; (2) they appeared to be juvenile age-wise; and (3) they were black. This questionnaire was prompted from investigators' weekly meetings that reported an increase of other gangs in the reported "active" neighborhoods, popular handouts. Investigators deduced from other gangs one group that had been ignored and continues to be ignored by traditional criminal justice researchers.

1. Are there any female crews in Detroit (all female or mixed)?

Yes	14
No answer	11
All-female	14

2. Any other type of gangs that you heard of besides Gang C-1?

All kinds	23
No answer	2

3. How would you describe this gang?

Everybody's in a crew— all the fellas got crews	9
Dope boys	7
Rap boys got crews	6
Everybody on our side of town gotta crew—Even the sissies gotta crew. Some sell dope, some getting paid for whacking mugs and some just out here doing whatever!	6

4. Are you a member of a crew?

Yes	4
No	13
No answer	8

5. Do gangs you know carry weapons?

Yes	23
No answer	2

6. Have you seen any gangs (crews) here today?

Yes	7
No answer	17

7. Do you fear any female crews?

Yes	4
No answer	21

8. Are there gangs at your school?

Yes	13
No answer	12

9. Would your parent(s) be upset if you joined a gang?

Yes	17
No answer	8

10. Do you know of any females who work for male gangs?

Yes	16
No	9

TABLE 5

Individual Female Interviews Between
June 1986 and August 1988

1. **Ages of the interviewees**

12	8
13	15
14	11
15	21
16	13
17	9
18	10
19	9
20	4

2. **Do you belong to a female gang?**

Yes	32
No	55
No answer	13

3. **Do you know male gangs?**

Yes	100

4. **Have you been involved in any violent acts through gangs?**

Yes	73
No	4
No answer	23

5. **Do you socialize with gang members (male or female)?**

Yes	54
No	3
Sometimes	16
No answer	30

6. **Do you attend school?**

Yes	78
No	12
Sometimes	10

7. **Do you use drugs?**

Yes	23
No	21
No answer	56

8. Do you sell drugs?
Yes   34
No answer   66

9. Do you own a gun or other weapon?
Yes   87
No   13

10. Do you own a car or scooter?
Yes   33
No   26
No answer   41

11. Do you have a job?
Yes*   42
No   59

---

*Part-time, mostly in fast food chains.

TABLE 6

Females Interviewed in a Group Session
July 1987

All-female gangs/groups; individuals; or non-gang/group individual females. A hundred were interviewed. Ninety of these were individuals. The following statistics were from the gang/group of ten.

1. **Does it matter if a guy is in a crew or not (as a friend)?**
   Yes   0
   No   10

2. **Does your parent(s) mind who you socialize with?**
   Yes   0
   No   10

3. **Are females as tough as guys (in general ways?)**
   Yes   10
   No   0
   (See female gang comments)

4. **Could your boyfriend belong to a crew?**
   Yes   8
   No   0
   No answer   2

5. **Do you know of any females who work
   with or for any male crews?**
   Yes   8
   No   0
   No Answer   2

6. **Do females that you know use drugs?**
   Yes   4
   No   0
   No answer   6

7. **Have you thought about marriage and children?**
   Yes   2
   No   0
   No answer   8

8. Is college in your future?

Yes	1
No	0
No answer	9

9. Have you ever seen any acts of violence personally?

Yes	10
No	0

10. Do you attend church?

Often	0
Sometimes	1
Seldom	1
Never	8

TABLE 7

Gang Members, 20 in each group, were asked between 1983 and 1986 if they had ever heard of selected people or know what they did for a living? These individuals represented local and national leaders of education, law, entertainment, sports, and politics. Investigators asked three groups (1) Scavengers, (2) Corporate, and at a later period, (3) Females.

	Scavenger	Corporate	Female
1. Thurgood Marshall	0	0	0
2. Vernon Jordan	0	0	0
3. Coleman Young	20	20	20
4. Whitney Young	0	0	0
5. Malcolm X	3	2	9
6. Martin Luther King, Jr.	5	4	14
7. Quincy Jones	13	15	17
8. John Coltrane	0	0	2
9. Stevie Wonder	20	20	20
10. Muhammad Ali	16	20	20
11. Thomas Hearns	20	20	20
12. Sugar Ray Robinson	0	12	9
13. Leon Spinks	3	11	15
14. Michael Jackson	20	20	20
15. Prince	20	20	20
16. Larry Holmes	2	11	19
17. Ronald Reagan	14	16	20
18. John Conyers	3	2	16
19. Emmanuel Stewart	2	9	14
20. Billie Holiday	0	0	3
21. Dinah Washington	0	0	3
22. Carmen McRae	0	0	2
23. Betty Carter	0	0	3
24. Barbara Jordan	0	0	0
25. Cicely Tyson	0	0	7
26. Ella Fitzgerald	3	2	13
27. Sarah Vaughn	0	1	13
28. Aretha Franklin	20	20	20
29. Erma Henderson	8	13	19
30. Marian Anderson	0	0	0

	Scavenger	Corporate	Female
31. Diana Ross	17	20	20
32. Lena Horne	0	0	3
33. Dayna Eubanks	13	11	18
34. Kathy Adams	15	11	20
35. Carmen Harlan	6	4	7
36. Coretta Scott King	3	0	8
37. Dr. Betty Shabazy	0	0	0
38. Jody Watley	20	20	20
39. Judge Damon Keith	6	4	17
40. Wiliam Hart	5	18	20
41. John L. Johnson	0	0	0
42. Earl Graves	0	0	0
43. Thomas "Beans" Bowles	0	2	9
44. Earl Van Dyke	6	11	12
45. Ernie Rodgers	9	13	17
46. Billy Sims	0	9	11
47. Gil Hill	4	16	18
48. Sammy Davis, Jr.	3	3	5
49. Arthur Ashe	0	0	3
50. Clifton R. Wharton, Jr.	0	0	0
51. Billy Bruton	0	0	0
52. Willie Horton	0	0	5
53. Dave Bing	0	0	3
54. Berry Gordy	0	0	7
55. Isiah Thomas	20	20	20
56. Marvin Gaye	18	20	20
57. Levi Stubbs	3	2	11
58. Susan L. Taylor	5	1	13
59. Bettye Lackey	0	0	0
60. Pam Grier	3	2	4
61. Rosa Parks	2	3	9
62. James Baldwin	0	0	3
63. Gwendolyn Brooks	0	0	0
64. Barbara Rose-Collins	8	4	11
65. Mary Wilson	2	0	4
66. Marva Collins	0	0	3
67. Carolyn Cheeks-Kilpatrick	0	0	2
68. Joyce Garcett	0	0	0
69. Mother Waddles	2	3	5
70. Florence Ballard	0	0	0

		Scavenger	Corporate	Female
71.	Betty DeRamus	0	0	4
72.	Verna Green	0	0	0
73.	Susan Watson	0	0	2
74.	Zina Garrison	0	0	0
75.	Eloise Whitten	0	0	0
76.	Wendy Baxter	0	0	8
77.	Robert Millender	0	0	0
78.	John Conyers	20	20	20
79.	George Crockett, Jr.	0	2	12
80.	Samuel Gardner	13	16	20
81.	Ed Bell	12	17	20
82.	William Milliken	0	0	0
83.	Rev. Nicolas Hood	0	0	2
84.	Rev. John Peoples	2	11	16
85.	Otis Culpepper	3	20	20
86.	Jesse Jackson	20	20	20
87.	Nathan Conyers	0	0	3
88.	James Blanchard	3	2	12
89.	Richard Austin	0	0	3
90.	John Eliott	0	0	0
91.	Rev. Wendell Anthony	5	3	9
92.	Rev. Charles Nicks	7	8	11
93.	Rev. Charles Adams	0	0	0
94.	John Porter	0	0	0
95.	Joe Hoskins	12	16	18
96.	Phyliss Hyman	2	3	13
97.	Toni Morrison	0	0	0
98.	Nettie Harris	0	0	0
99.	Vanity	19	16	19
100.	Geraldine B. Ford	4	3	12
101.	Fidel Castro	0	0	0
102.	Alma Stallworth	3	6	9
103.	Kim Weston	6	5	3
104.	Dolores Wharton	0	0	0
105.	Mahalia Jackson	0	0	0
106.	Camille Cosby	0	0	0
107.	Clarice Taylor	0	0	0
108.	Janet Jackson	20	20	20
109.	Kim Fields	20	20	20
110.	Debbie Allen	13	9	10

	Scavenger	Corporate	Female
111. LaToya Jackson	20	20	20
112. Phyllica Ayers-Allen	11	13	17
113. Reggie Jackson	0	6	13
114. Keisha Knight Pulliam	0	0	12
115. Lisa Bonet	3	18	19
116. Arthur Jefferson	2	1	14
117. Ed Bradley	0	1	13
118. Myzell Sowell	0	6	8
119. Gerald Evelyn	0	4	6
120. Lester Hudson	0	3	14
121. Eddie Murphy	20	20	20
122. Gregory Hines	7	8	15
123. Bryant Gumbel	13	15	20
124. Irene Graves	0	0	0
125. LaBarbara Gragg	0	0	0
126. Georgia Brown	0	0	0
127. Joe Falls	0	0	2
128. Larry Bird	2	20	20
129. Pete Waldmeir	0	0	0
130. Jimmy Carter	0	0	5
131. Magic Johnson	20	20	20
132. Andrew Young	0	0	3
133. Henry Ford II	10	13	20
134. Jackie Wilson	0	0	3
135. Dick Clark	20	16	20
136. Don Cornelius	20	20	20
137. S. Martin Taylor	0	0	2
138. Gladys Barsimian	9	16	18
139. Maryann Maheffy	2	1	11
140. Ray Charles	4	7	9
141. Jim Brown	0	0	1
142. Prince Charles of Great Britain	6	2	9
143. Nat "King" Cole	0	0	3
144. B. B. King	3	8	9
145. Althea Gibson	0	0	2
146. Jackie Robinson	0	0	3
147. Sam Cook	0	0	3
148. Wilt Chamberlain	0	2	5
149. Bill Russell	0	0	1
150. Miles Davis	1	3	6

	Scavenger	Corporate	Female
151. Lee Iococca	20	20	20
152. Kirk Gibson	0	9	16
153. Harold Washington	0	0	2
154. Clyde Cleveland	6	13	15
155. Sparky Anderson	4	17	20

Dangerous Society

Production Editor: Julie L. Loehr
Design: Lynne A. Brown
Copy Editors: Martha A. Bates and
                Jo Grandstaff
Proofreader: Kristine M. Blakeslee
Text composed by: the Copyfitters, Ltd.

Printed by Thomson-Shore, Inc.
on 60# Finch Opaque with
Rainbow Antique Charcoal A endsheets

Smyth sewn and cased
in Holliston Crown Design Linen
Grotto Green